A brief account of the dreadful fire at Blandford-Forum ... which happened June iv. M.DCC.XXXI. Together with a sermon preached at Blandford, June 4, 1735. ... By Malachi Blake. The second edition.

Malachi Blake

A brief account of the dreadful fire at Blandford-Forum ... which happened June iv. M.DCC.XXXI. Together with a sermon preached at Blandford, June 4, 1735. ... By Malachi Blake. The second edition.
Blake, Malachi
ESTCID: T117186
Reproduction from British Library

London : printed for the author, and sold by R. Ford ; and A. Tozer bookseller in Exon., 1735.
viii,108p.,plate : map ; 12°

Eighteenth Century
Collections Online
Print Editions

Gale ECCO Print Editions

Relive history with *Eighteenth Century Collections Online*, now available in print for the independent historian and collector. This series includes the most significant English-language and foreign-language works printed in Great Britain during the eighteenth century, and is organized in seven different subject areas including literature and language; medicine, science, and technology; and religion and philosophy. The collection also includes thousands of important works from the Americas.

The eighteenth century has been called "The Age of Enlightenment." It was a period of rapid advance in print culture and publishing, in world exploration, and in the rapid growth of science and technology – all of which had a profound impact on the political and cultural landscape. At the end of the century the American Revolution, French Revolution and Industrial Revolution, perhaps three of the most significant events in modern history, set in motion developments that eventually dominated world political, economic, and social life.

In a groundbreaking effort, Gale initiated a revolution of its own: digitization of epic proportions to preserve these invaluable works in the largest online archive of its kind. Contributions from major world libraries constitute over 175,000 original printed works. Scanned images of the actual pages, rather than transcriptions, recreate the works ***as they first appeared.***

Now for the first time, these high-quality digital scans of original works are available via print-on-demand, making them readily accessible to libraries, students, independent scholars, and readers of all ages.

For our initial release we have created seven robust collections to form one the world's most comprehensive catalogs of 18th century works.

Initial Gale ECCO Print Editions collections include:

> ***History and Geography***
> Rich in titles on English life and social history, this collection spans the world as it was known to eighteenth-century historians and explorers. Titles include a wealth of travel accounts and diaries, histories of nations from throughout the world, and maps and charts of a world that was still being discovered. Students of the War of American Independence will find fascinating accounts from the British side of conflict.

Social Science
Delve into what it was like to live during the eighteenth century by reading the first-hand accounts of everyday people, including city dwellers and farmers, businessmen and bankers, artisans and merchants, artists and their patrons, politicians and their constituents. Original texts make the American, French, and Industrial revolutions vividly contemporary.

Medicine, Science and Technology
Medical theory and practice of the 1700s developed rapidly, as is evidenced by the extensive collection, which includes descriptions of diseases, their conditions, and treatments. Books on science and technology, agriculture, military technology, natural philosophy, even cookbooks, are all contained here.

Literature and Language
Western literary study flows out of eighteenth-century works by Alexander Pope, Daniel Defoe, Henry Fielding, Frances Burney, Denis Diderot, Johann Gottfried Herder, Johann Wolfgang von Goethe, and others. Experience the birth of the modern novel, or compare the development of language using dictionaries and grammar discourses.

Religion and Philosophy
The Age of Enlightenment profoundly enriched religious and philosophical understanding and continues to influence present-day thinking. Works collected here include masterpieces by David Hume, Immanuel Kant, and Jean-Jacques Rousseau, as well as religious sermons and moral debates on the issues of the day, such as the slave trade. The Age of Reason saw conflict between Protestantism and Catholicism transformed into one between faith and logic -- a debate that continues in the twenty-first century.

Law and Reference
This collection reveals the history of English common law and Empire law in a vastly changing world of British expansion. Dominating the legal field is the *Commentaries of the Law of England* by Sir William Blackstone, which first appeared in 1765. Reference works such as almanacs and catalogues continue to educate us by revealing the day-to-day workings of society.

Fine Arts
The eighteenth-century fascination with Greek and Roman antiquity followed the systematic excavation of the ruins at Pompeii and Herculaneum in southern Italy; and after 1750 a neoclassical style dominated all artistic fields. The titles here trace developments in mostly English-language works on painting, sculpture, architecture, music, theater, and other disciplines. Instructional works on musical instruments, catalogs of art objects, comic operas, and more are also included.

The BiblioLife Network

This project was made possible in part by the BiblioLife Network (BLN), a project aimed at addressing some of the huge challenges facing book preservationists around the world. The BLN includes libraries, library networks, archives, subject matter experts, online communities and library service providers. We believe every book ever published should be available as a high-quality print reproduction; printed on-demand anywhere in the world. This insures the ongoing accessibility of the content and helps generate sustainable revenue for the libraries and organizations that work to preserve these important materials.

The following book is in the "public domain" and represents an authentic reproduction of the text as printed by the original publisher. While we have attempted to accurately maintain the integrity of the original work, there are sometimes problems with the original work or the micro-film from which the books were digitized. This can result in minor errors in reproduction. Possible imperfections include missing and blurred pages, poor pictures, markings and other reproduction issues beyond our control. Because this work is culturally important, we have made it available as part of our commitment to protecting, preserving, and promoting the world's literature.

GUIDE TO FOLD-OUTS MAPS and OVERSIZED IMAGES

The book you are reading was digitized from microfilm captured over the past thirty to forty years. Years after the creation of the original microfilm, the book was converted to digital files and made available in an online database.

In an online database, page images do not need to conform to the size restrictions found in a printed book. When converting these images back into a printed bound book, the page sizes are standardized in ways that maintain the detail of the original. For large images, such as fold-out maps, the original page image is split into two or more pages

Guidelines used to determine how to split the page image follows:

- Some images are split vertically; large images require vertical and horizontal splits.
- For horizontal splits, the content is split left to right.
- For vertical splits, the content is split from top to bottom.
- For both vertical and horizontal splits, the image is processed from top left to bottom right.

A BRIEF ACCOUNT OF THE DREADFUL FIRE

AT

BLANDFORD-FORUM

IN THE

County of DORSET, which happened *June* iv. M.DCC XXXI.

Together with a

SERMON

Preached at *Blandford, June* 4. 1735. being the Day set apart by the *Protestant Dissenters* there for Prayer and Humiliation under the Remembrance of that SAD PROVIDENCE.

To which is added,

A SERIOUS ADDRESS to the Inhabitants of that Town.

By *MALACHI BLAKE*.

The SECOND EDITION.

Suppose ye that these Galileans *were Sinners above all the* Galileans, *because they suffered such Things? I tell you nay: But except ye repent ye shall all likewise perish,*
Luke xiii. 2, 3.

Rebus angustis animosus atque
Fortis appare :   *Hor. Lib.* ii. *Ode* x.
Quantò quisque sibi plura negaverit,
A Diis plura feret.   *Hor. Lib.* iii. *Ode* xvi.

This Treatise is not only calculated for the Inhabitants of *Blandford*, but proper for other Families also.

London, *Printed for the Author, and sold by* R. Ford, *in the Poultry, and* A. Tozer *Bookseller in* Exon. 1735   Price Stitch'd One Shilling, Bound One Shilling and Three Pence.

THE PREFACE.

HAT the Memory of such an unusual and solemn Event as the late dreadful Fire at Blandford may be perpetuated, and that we and others may be assisted to make such proper Reflections thereon, as may tend to advance the Honour and Glory of God, and our real Good; it has been the Opinion of many that some Account of it should be published to the World.

To this End, some Time after the Calamity, *I drew up a Relation thereof, with some* Exhortations *suitable to the* Case, *and thought to have made them publick sooner, but could not prevail with my self to do so. I debated this Matter so long in my own Mind, that the* Objection *arising from its* Unseasonableness, *which every Week and Day seemed to gather new Strength, became almost* insuperable; *and this as well as other* Objections *against my appearing in* Print *had a particular* Influence *on me, it being much more agreeable to my own* Inclinations *to pass through the World more* silently.

However, seeing no Person had taken upon him to tell the World the doleful Story, several of my Friends (that wished to see some Account

Account of our severe Affliction made publick, together with some practical Reflections *and* Monitions *suitable to the Nature of it) knowing that I had entertained some Thoughts this way, laid hold of every Opportunity to renew their Requests for my prosecuting my Design, and pressed me with many Arguments. Now, though the earnest* Solicitations *of my Friends had their Weight with me, yet, I think I can say after all, that the most prevailing and determining Argument to send forth into the World the following Tracts was, a* Consciousness *of* Duty, *arising from the* uncommon *and* tremendous *Nature of the Providence, my Situation here, and my Obligation thereupon, to employ, not my* Tongue *only, but my* Pen *also towards the right Improvement of it.*

I

The Preface.

I am very sensible that the Seasonableness of any Tract contributes much to its Acceptableness; and that it is a Part of Wisdom to choose the fittest Season; *and whether* this Time *is yet* past, *I will not dispute, some think not:* However it may (by the Blessing of God) be now *as* useful *to* others, *as it may help to revive in them a Sense of* God's awful Providence; *and be, perhaps, as* seasonable *and as* serviceable *to* this Town, *who are now more at* Leisure *to consider calmly and sedately of* God's *Dealings with us, than in the* hurrying Months *that are past.* No chastening for the present seems joyous but grievous; nevertheless afterward it yieldeth the peaceable Fruits of Righteousness unto them which are exercised there-

thereby, *Heb.* xii. 11. *After the Relation of the dismal Story of* the Fire, *which I have endeavoured to throw together in such a Manner, as I hope will offend none, gratify some,* inform, *and do* Good *to others,* I have (*that I may rouse and keep alive in Men a more deep and affecting Sense of* God's awful *and awakening Dispensations, which I apprehend is a Matter of vast Importance*) added hereunto a plain and practical Sermon *on the great* Doctrine *of* Providence. *And standing more immediately related to some, who for many Years past have been under my* Ministerial Care ; *and to* others *on the Score of* Friendship *and mutual* Sufferings, *I have judg'd it proper to conclude the Whole with a serious and earnest* Address

or

or Exhortation *to the* Inhabitants *in general. And I please my self with the Hopes, that this Treatise may be useful to* others *also, particularly to such as have very lately, or within a few Years past, suffered by the like Calamity;* as Dorchester, Gravesend, Stowerminster, Henstridge, Tiverton, Ramsey, &c.

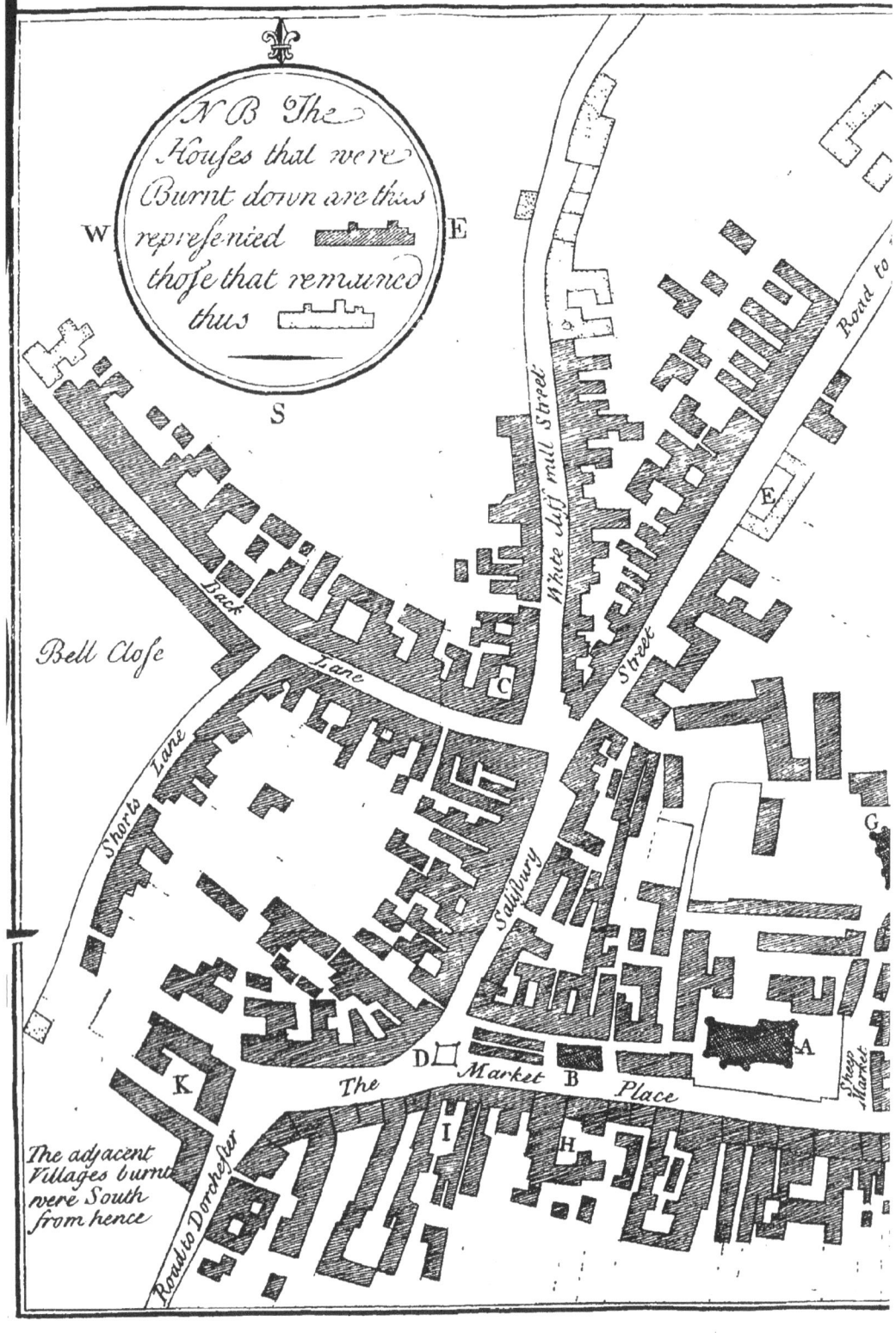

A BRIEF ACCOUNT OF THE FIRE at *Blandford*.

THE wonderful *Works* of God, whether of *Mercy* or of *Judgment*, ought to be had in *Remembrance*, especially by those immediately concerned in them; yea, a Remembrance of them ought to be conveyed down from one Generation to another; according to that in the Prophet, *Hear this ye old Men, and give Ear all ye Inhabitants of the Land: Hath this been in your Days, or even in the Days of your Fathers? Tell ye your Children of it, and let your Children tell their Children, and their*

Children another Generation [a]. It is mentioned as Matter of *Reproach* to the *Israelites*, and as a very *provoking* Sin, that *they* remember'd *not God's Hand;* yea, *they soon forgat his Works* [b]. Whereas a due *Regard* to his *providential* Dispensations is the Way to his Favour. *Thou meetest him,* with thy tender Mercies, *that worketh Righteousness, those that remember thee in thy Ways* [c].

Now, that a *Sense* of God's *rebuking Hand* may remain fresh *in our own* Minds, and that *others* also may learn the Lesson he expects from it; I have, upon the best Information I could get, thrown together, in a short Compass, a true, but very melancholy *Account* of that general CONFLAGRATION which happened amongst us on *Friday, June* the Fourth, 1731.

About Two of the Clock in the *Afternoon* a *dismal Cry* of *Fire* was heard in our Streets. The *Inhabitants* of the Place were all soon alarmed; some were called from their *Business;* some, possibly, from their *Pleasures;* some, perhaps, from their *Cups:* However, every one was *terribly surprized;* though those one would hope

[a] Joel i. 2, 3.   [b] Psal. lxxviii. 42. and cvi. 13.
[c] Isa. lxiv. 5.

were in the best Posture and Temper of Mind to bear it, who were most *usefully* or *innocently* imployed.

The Fire *first kindled* on the *Out-side* of a *Soap-boiler*'s House, occasioned (as he conjectures) by Sparks that fell from a Chimney upon the Thatch. Some think differently, but all agree, that as to Man it was intirely *accidental*. —— The *House* stood on rising Ground where *four Streets met*, not far from the Middle of the Town. Our three *Engines* were soon brought out and play'd, but to no Purpose, for in little more than half an Hour they either were all burnt or render'd unfit for Service.

The *Wind*, which sat *North-West*, quickly carried the Fire into distant Parts. *Every Corner* of these four Streets were presently in Flames that raged onward, *with*, and *against* the Wind. —— The *Fire* spread it self with that *speed* and *fury*, that every Thing was soon devoured before it. Not a Piece of *Timber* but what was burnt to a *Coal*. The *Pewter* in many Houses was not only melted, but reduced to *Ashes* by the fervent Heat. Our *Silver*, in a literal Sense, became Dross! And if any made *fine Gold* their *Confidence*, what a sad Proof had they before their Eyes, of their extreme *Folly*, and its *utter Infufficiency* to make them *happy!*

Moſt Perſons (which was very obſervable) were at once *ſeized* with ſuch a *Panic*, that they gave up the *Town for loſt*, quickly after the Fire broke out. *What ail'd thee, O thou Fire, that thou waſt ſo ſtrong? That nothing could drive thee back?* Was it not becauſe thou hadſt thy Commiſſion from *above?* Surely we have ſeen, we have felt thy Power, O Lord! Ah, who can ſtand before God when once he is angry?

Before *Seven of the Clock* in the Evening (which was about *four Hours* after the Fire began) there was ſcarce an Houſe remained, but what, at leaſt, was ſo much in Flames, as to be paſt the Reach of Men to preſerve it; except ſome *few*, which Providence reſerved, as in Kindneſs to the Owners, ſo in Pity to them who had *none left*.

A neighbouring *Hamlet* (at ſome conſiderable Diſtance, and on the other Side of the River, in the Pariſhes of St. *Mary-Blandford*, and *Brianſton*) was almoſt totally *conſumed* alſo, occaſioned by ſome Flakes of Fire, carried from us, and falling on their Thatch'd Buildings. —— Only three Houſes were ſaved in that *Hamlet*; the *Preſervation* of which, conſidering their

Situ-

Situation, and the *Danger* they were in, was *surprizing* to all that *then* beheld them, or have since seen them.

Some *few Houses* were remarkably preserved at the *four Quarters* of the Town (as you may see in the prefixed *Plan*) which we would ascribe chiefly to a *good Providence*; *The Lord said, it is enough, and the Fire was stayed!* Yet we would not forget the kind and the timely *Assistance* of such as came from several Parts of the *Country*, though they were indeed *too late* to *attempt* any Service for those who lived *farther in the Town*. —— A neighbouring *Gentleman* also, upon the first Notice he had of our Distress, came with the utmost Speed to afford us (according to his *wonted Humanity*) his best Offices; *perswading* some, and *hiring* others by *present* or *promised* Rewards, to help us. So that to his prudent Management, Direction and Care, it was much owing (under God) that the Fire ceased at *two* of the Quarters. —— I would not pass by here, what, we may presume, was no small Reason in Providence that there was not now an intire Desolation; I mean the *fervent Prayers of many, that God would stay his Hand*. For, at this Time, *almost every one* join'd in *one common and earnest Cry* unto Heaven for

Mercy.

Mercy. God heard our Cry, and his Bowels were moved for us.

The Fire *ceased* at the *East Part* of the Town, where the last great Fire *began*; which was on the Ninth Day of *July*, 1713. *Then* all those Houses which now escaped were burnt down to the Ground, to the further End of the Street. So that in so small a Tract of Time, as within the Space of *Twenty Years*, there's scarce an *House* now *standing* which has not been *rebuilt*.

In the Day of our great Calamity, so *sudden* was the Fire, so *furious*, that *many* Families had scarce Time to save *any* of their Effects; few had either Time or Help to save *much* 'Tis true, much *Household Goods*, as well as all Sorts of *Merchandise*, were in the *Beginning* carried to *distant Houses*, where it was then apprehended they were safe from Danger, and much was brought out into the *Streets*, in hopes of timely Assistance to convey it away. But, alas! they were soon sadly disappointed, and forced to leave to the devouring Flames, what they had with so much Pains and Difficulty brought thither. Many were now *thankful* they could escape with their own *Lives!* Or, however their *Hearts* might be disposed, they scarce had

had Time to look back on what they had left behind them! Which should teach us *to labour not for the Meat that perisheth, but for that which endureth unto everlasting Life* [d].

—— I shall never forget the Horror and *Affrightment* that appeared in every Countenance, render'd yet more *frightful* by the Labour and Toil of the Day. Many were *scarce known* even to their *nearest Neighbours*, so disfigured were they with Sorrow, Smoke, and Soot! For, alas! *The Day of the Lord was come; as a Destruction from the Almighty it came upon us* [e].

And yet *new Surprizes*, and *more bitter Anguish* seize the Hearts of many. In BLANDFORD *there was a Voice heard, Lamentation and Weeping, and great Mourning:* Many, like *Rachel* of old, *weeping for their Children, and would not be comforted, because* they thought *they were not* [f]. How many Parents, with the most afflicting Solicitude, were searching here and there for their lost Children! neither knowing where to find them, nor (for many Hours together) so much as hoping ever to see them alive again! *Their Fears* strongly *suggesting* to them that their *little ones* were *devoured* in the torturing Flames. Shocking Thought! But it pleased the *Father of Mercies*, by a

[d] John vi. 27.   [e] Isai. xiii. 6.   [f] Matt. ii. 18.

singu-

singular Direction of Providence, to *take care* of those poor *wandring Lambs*, some flying for Refuge to one Place, some to another: Insomuch that before the Morning, they were *all* (for not one Child perished in the Flames) happily restored, not indeed to their Fathers *Houses* (for Houses they had none) but to the *transporting Sight*, and most *endearing Embraces* of their *revived Parents*; who no sooner fasten their Eyes on these dear Creatures, but they shed, even for Joy, the few Tears they had left; gladly catching them into their Arms, as being *all* they could now *call their own*.

But, alas! *that Joy*, like every Thing else in this vain Life, was soon *swallowed up* in fresh *Sorrows*. Though when they looked upon their rescued Children, it *pleased* them much that none of them were *lost*; yet to think they had lost the *Labours* of many Years, and *that* by which they hoped to have made comfortable Provision for them, this *sunk their Spirits* again, and became a new Source of Grief. And yet *more Grief* behind! Their Children cry for Bread to satisfy their Hunger, and for *Drink* to quench their Thirst. As for *Bread*, their Parents, alas! had *none*; and could not for their *Drink* easily procure them so much as *Water*. They cried for *Houses* also so to lodge in, and for Beds to lie on; but very few could help them to either. Happy they, who, in such deep Distress as this, could take comfort in our Saviour's Words, *Let not your Hearts be troubled; in my Father's House are many* MANSIONS [g].

The dismal *Night* comes on; when *many* who were never inured to Hardship were obliged to lie, *some* in *Barns* and *Out-Houses*; others under the *Arches* of a large *Bridge*; and more under *Hedges* and in the *open Air*.

The *Church* held out against the Fury of the Flames a long Time, not having any House joining to it. At length the *Steeple* took Fire, and that more than once; but by the great Care and Diligence of some Persons it was quenched again. However, about *Twelve of the Clock at Night*, the Fire was seen afresh in the *Middle* of the *Roof*. This also might have been stopped at first had they had *Engines*, or could they have got *Ladders* and *Vessels* to carry Water: But these were all burnt. It was towards *Two of the Clock in the Morning* before it broke through the Roof into a *Flame*. Then the *Fire roared* dreadfully, the *Lead melted*, the *Stones split* and *flew*; nay, so fervent and irresistible was the Heat, that the

---

[g] John xiv. 1.

Bells themselves *diſſolved* and ran *down in Streams*.

It was a *Mercy*, however, that this *ſpacious Pile of Building* was burnt *no ſooner*; for ſeveral who had carried their Goods into it, and betook themſelves for Shelter within its Walls, were not able for ſome Time, without great Hazard of their Lives, either to *retreat* from, or to *bear* the ſcorching [...] from the Houſes that were burning [...] it Whilſt others were glad to [lie down] behind the *Tomb-Stones*, which [caſt a] *Shadow* to them from the fervent Heat *on one Side*, as the Church it ſelf was *on the other*, until the Fire about it was ſo far abated as to give them *Opportunity* to ſave themſelves, and to carry off the Effects they had with them.

In other Calamities the *Deſcription* commonly *exceeds* the *Truth*; but ours was ſuch that it *ſurpaſſed* all the *Repreſentations* that have ever been made of it.

A Town, which the other Day was ſo *agreeable* to its *Inhabitants*, and to *Strangers* that paſſed through it, can't now be *looked upon* without *Horror*, nor be *paſſed through* without *Danger*. Now the *Feet* that walk therein are even *ſcorched* with burning Heat; and Perſons are obliged to look narrowly about them, as they haſte along, leſt *bowing Walls* and *tottering*

tering Chimnies (which appeared at a Distance like craggy Rocks) should, being deprived of their usual Supports, fall upon them, and *encrease* the mournful *Number* of those that were already dead. —— A continual *Fire* and *Smoke* for some Days (fed by the *Remains* of ruined Houses, and those *Stores* of *Wood* and *Coal* the Inhabitants had laid up for their Winter Fewel) were *vomited out*, as from so many *subterraneous Volcano's*: So that it might be truly said of this Place, *The Lord poured out his fierce Anger, and kindled a Fire therein, and it hath devoured the Foundations thereof*[h]. But to return;

All the *following Night*, while the Fire was slowly abating, *some* were employed in *keeping Watch* over the few *Houses* that were spared; others in *searching* after their lost *Relations* and *Children*. Some of their Friends they found dead in the Streets, part of them consumed with the Flames, while the *melancholy Remains* of them were burnt Black as an Hearth, and even roasted in the Fire. These *Remains* of human Bodies which they now found, together with others which after some Days were dug out from under the Ruins of Houses, some in one Place, some in another, that

[h] Lam. iv. 11.

by Circumstances they *guessed* to be the *Relicks* of their dead *Relatives*, they carried to the usual *Place of Burial* for their more decent Interment.

The *Number* of those that *perished* has been generally reckoned to be *Sixteen*; but upon the best Inquiry I could make I can't find they were more than *Thirteen*; not one Child (as has been already observ'd) but most of them *aged Persons*, viz. *three Men* and *ten Women*. ⸺ One of those who were burnt to Death was seen at a Distance endeavouring to make her Escape. She soon dropt down, her Cloaths being on Fire about her. The Person who saw her could not with *Safety* attempt her Preservation, she being encompass'd with Flames. ⸺ *Another*, in like Danger, was seasonably rescued by her Son, who went with a Friend of his to seek after her. They espied her at some Distance in the Street, surrounded with Smoke and Fire. At first they were *afraid* to come near, thinking it impracticable to save *her* and *themselves* too. However her *Son* at last *ventured*, took her by the Arm, and they brought her off the least dangerous Way they could see, through a Gate-House that soon after fell down. All *three* were mercifully preserved ⸺ *Another* who had but little Hopes of saving himself, as he he was *hurrying* along, an *aged Woman* earnestly *craved* his *Help*. He desired her to hold fast by the *Skirt* of his Coat, which she did, till he had helped her on so far that he presumed she had been safe. But being in so much Danger himself, he had neither *Time* nor *Power* to be any longer thoughtful about her, for he had gone but a little farther e'er the Heat was so strong that it took away his Breath. He dropt down, and was unable to rise again; but was taken up by one that opportunely came by, and his Life was saved; while the poor Woman (to whom he had afforded all the good Offices he was able in his then dangerous Circumstances) was burnt in the Street. ——— *Another Man*, apprehending that *his Wife* and *his Child* (tho' safe elsewhere) had been left in his House, when it was in Flames, (tortur'd, no doubt, with *different Passions*, Love to his Wife and Child, *Fear* of losing his own Life, with *Hopes* that by a bold Attempt all might be preserved) ventured in, and (after he had found his Mistake) with great Hazard made his Escape out again, being almost scorched to Death. ——— A *Gentleman* of the Town returning from the Place where the Fire first began, to his own House, was unexpectedly surrounded with Flames. After he had *passed* the Fire at *one Place* he came to *another* that was *impassable*; so that he was obliged to make his Retreat with the utmost Danger of his Life, being miserably burnt. Soon after this he made the best of his Way over the River, into the Parish of St. *Mary-Blandford*, to a Friend's House there, and having anointed his Hands and his Face with some Oil, he laid himself down upon the Bed. But, alas! in a very short Time *that Place* was in Flames also, and he was forced to seek for Refuge elsewhere. Restless World indeed! *Happy they who have a Rest remaining for them in a better.*

Many others were in the *greatest Danger*, running for their Lives through the Streets, scarce able to keep themselves on their Legs, holding Handkerchiefs up to their Faces to keep their Breath, and to defend them from the scorching Heat; while *others* leaped out of Windows to save themselves, no other Way being left for their Deliverance. What *Multitudes* must have perished had the Calamity happened in the Night! Good God, we bless thee that *in the Midst of Judgment thou didst remember Mercy.*

One of the *Surgeons* of this Place returning out of the Country whilst the Town was on Fire, ventured into the *Heart* of
it

it in quest of his aged Mother (his House being situated there) and was so scorched with the Flames, that for some Time he needed the Assistance he would gladly have afforded: While another Gentleman of the same Profession had his *Person* and his *House* both kindly and providentially *preserved*, many needing his Help and his *Medicines* too, to mitigate their torturing Pains. He had upwards of *Fifty* under his Care at once, who all recovered, tho' some of them were burnt to that degree, and their Pains were so exquisite, that they could have wished themselves out of this afflicting World.—— What *Scenes* of *Sorrow* were *opened* in a *few Hours*! How many *weeping Eyes* and bleeding Hearts! We have often read, *That Man is born unto Trouble, as the Sparks fly upward*[i]; but never *experienced this* so sensibly as now. Shall we any more *say in our Prosperity, we shall never be moved*[k]?

The *Small Pox* at the same Time *prevailed* in the Town. This render'd the *other Calamity* doubly afflictive to the Houses in which it was. About *Sixty* Families, by Computation, were then visited with that Distemper. *Not one* indeed of the Sick *perished* in the *Flames*; but then

[i] Job v. 7.   [k] Psal. xxx. 6.

they were many of them *exposed* to the greatest Hazard other ways. Some *little ones* in this hurrying Time were snatched up out of their *Beds,* and carried away *without any Thing almost about them,* so that their *tender Mothers* were forced to *strip* themselves of part of their *necessary* Garments to cover them. And in this *diseased* and *exposed* Condition *some* Persons were laid in the *open Fields, some* under *Hedges,* and the *Arches* of the Bridge, intermixed with *those* that but a little before *fled* from the *Infection.* ——— *Some,* who were down of the Distemper and left in their Beds (in this Time of general Confusion) by those that attended them, were soon *roused* with the dreadful *Cry of Fire,* and its roaring Flames; who in the Fright *tore open* their Eyes to see their Danger, and make their Escape, and wrapping up themselves in part of their Bed-Cloaths, made the best Speed their weak State would admit of, into the *Gardens* for Security: And yet though they had for some Time no shelter there but what the Hedges or Trees afforded them, they recovered.

Others, when the Fire *drew near* their Dwellings, *carried off* their sick *Children* and *Friends* to *distant Houses,* for greater Safety. But no sooner had they *quieted* themselves

selves a little with this *imaginary Escape*, and with the Hopes of gaining by this Means, a little Time, to save a *Part* of their Goods, but they were *again alarm'd* with the sad Tidings, that the Fire had seized *those Houses* also. And now they are brought to *yeild* to what they could not at first think of without *Horror*, viz. to carry their Sick into the open Fields, and were thankful they could thus save them from the devouring Flames. It is well, considering what a World we live in, that *human Nature* is so framed, that oftentimes some *greater Troubles* seem to swallow up, or reconcile us unto *lesser ones*. That which once was the Object of our *Dread*, may, upon the Comparison, become desirable, and Matter of *Choice*.

The *Physicians*, in the mean Time, took the best Care of them they were able; and through the timely and benevolent Provision of some *Apothecaries* in this Town (who sent immediately to *Salisbury* and elsewhere for such Medicines as were most needed) they were soon tolerably supply'd: And within a Day or two after the Fire two or three *neighbouring Gentlemen* looked in upon us, and left *Forty Guineas* for the Relief of these and the other Sufferers. Such kind and *early Acts of Compassion* deserve our most *grateful Remembrance*.

Yet upon the Whole, our *Condition* was melancholy beyond *Expression*, our *Calamities* were great and numberless, those that appeared before in *Change* of Raiment now were *glad* even of *necessary* Garments, and those that lived *delicately*, and fared *sumptuously* every Day, were now thankful for a *Morsel of Bread*. As the Reverend Mr. *Pitt*, in a Poem lately published upon this *melancholy Subject*, represents our Case,

The Scarlet rob'd, who late on Dainties fed,
With their own Slaves partake the Gift of Bread.

The *Morning after the Fire* there was a great *Scarcity* of *Provision*. However, some Supplies were immediately thought of, and found. There were *two Ovens* full of Loaves, which were set in a little before the Fire began; *these*, though bak'd to a *Crust* (for the Houses were both burnt to which the Ovens belong'd) were very acceptable. But *before Night* we had fresh *Supplies* sent in from the *neighbouring Parishes*. —— The *Sabbath-Day* after the Fire, and for some Days following, *Waggon Loads* of *Bread* and *Beer*, with some *Flesh*, were kindly and liberally sent us from the Places about us; as from *Shaftsbury, Pool, Wimborne, Dorchester, Wareham, Beer,* &c. Among many others, a *neighbouring Gentle-*

Gentleman was so generous, as to send in considerable Quantities of *Wheat* and some fat *Oxen.* We were by this Time so very *desirous of Flesh*, we had scarce *Patience* to stay till it was *distributed* to us.

Liberal Collections were soon made in several of the *adjacent Towns*, and Sums of Money sent us from *private Hands; part* of which was given away (to some *more*, to others *less*) to buy *Utensils*, and such Things as were *necessary* for their several *Imployments. Part* also of this early Charity was laid out upon *Sheep* and *Swine;* which were killed and distributed twice a Week, in such Portions as were answerable to the Number of the Families that partook of them.

Care also was taken to build *Barracks*, for the Reception of such as lay exposed to the open Air. The *Number* of the Barracks was upwards of *Sixty.* They were built with *Boards;* and before the Winter drew on were *covered* with *Thatch.* Those who dwelt in them run up *Chimnies*, and stopt the *Crevices* with *Moss* and other Things. *Some Families* continue to reside in them to *this Day.* —— Large Sums were laid out in buying *Linen* and *Rugs*, and *Blankets*, for such as were in great Distress for want of them.—— *Four Hundred* Families were burnt *out*, and *many* of them
reduced

reduced to great *Extremity*, so that several hundred Pounds of the *publick Charity* were expended in their present Maintenance, and to put them in a Way towards the better subsisting themselves for the Future.

The *whole Loss* given in upon Oath (for every one was sworn to the Account that he brought in) over and above all *Insurances*, amounted to *eighty four Thousand three Hundred* and *forty eight Pounds*. —— Now lest any should imagine that the *Distributions* already made are much greater than they really are, it mayn't be improper to take Notice, that *hitherto* they have amounted to no more than *six Shillings to the Pound*. There remains one *Dividend* more to be made, arising from what was given to the *Briefs*, which will amount to no more than three Pence, or four Pence in the Pound; however, at most, it will not come up to six Pence in the Pound [1].

[1] *The* Trustees *appointed by Act of Parliament, are as follow*; *The Honourable* George Dodington, *Sir* William Napiper, *Sir* William Chapple, *Sir* James Thornhill, George Chaffin, Edmund Moreton Pleydell, William Portman, Henry Drax, George Trenchard, Richard Bingham, Robert Henley, William Churchill, John Dennet, Humphry Sturt, John Banks, Joshua Churchill, Robert Lewen, Robert Mitchell, Walter Ridout, *and* Robert Snooke.

As *several Persons* never received any Part of the *public* Charities at all, so *others* who received their Share of the *first Dividend* (which was only *two Shillings* to the Pound) were afterwards *excluded*, by an *Order* made at a Meeting of some of the *Trustees*, from having any further Share. But notwithstanding the *Distributions* have amounted to no more, *by reason of the Greatness of our Loss*, yet *great*, surprisingly great, was the *Bounty* of our *Fellow-Christians*. A most *remarkable Spirit* of Charity has been discovered in the *British Nation* upon this and such like Occasions. Where *Liberty* prevails most, the *Inhabitants* of such Countries, as they are most *capable* of, so we find they are most *inclined* to Acts of *generous Benevolence*.

Our *Calamities* soon reached the *Ears*, and touched the *Hearts* of Persons of *all Ranks* and *Orders* among us with the utmost Compassion; both which I cannot sum up in Terms more *pertinent* and *pathetic* than in those of the Reverend Mr. *Harris* of *Gravesend*, on the like mournful Occasion. —— " When we call to mind
" the Calamity that [lately] befel us;
" when we consider how unexpectedly it
" arose, how fast it gathered Strength,
" with what Progress it advanced, and
" what Desolation it carried along with
" it;

"it; how in a few Hours space it de-
"stroyed our Wealth and Possessions, and
"the Means and Effects of our Industry:
"When we remember the sudden Alte-
"ration that [a few Hours] made in the
"Condition and Fortunes of our Neigh-
"bours and Friends, driving out many of
"them naked and destitute, depriving
"them in an instant of their Habitations
"and Employments, and leaving them
"utterly at a Loss to provide for their
"daily Necessity, or where to *lay their
"Heads*. More especially when we con-
"sider the Desolation and Destruction
"that at the same Time, and by the same
"Means, befel the [Places of our reli-
"gious Assemblies;] that at that very
"Juncture, when we stood most in need
"of Assembling our selves together, and
"of confessing and bewailing our Iniqui-
"ties, and of vowing a better Obedience
"for the Time to come, and of hearing
"God speak — by his Ministers, that
"at that very Juncture, I say, we were
"deprived of these external Means both
"of Repentance and Consolation. When
"we remember and consider these Things,
"how justly may we apply to our selves
"the Words of the Psalmist, *In Chasten-
"ing the Lord hath chastened me*; or, *the
"Lord hath chastened me sore.*

"But

"But then the Words that follow are "no less applicable to our State and "Condition than the former; and we "can with equal Justice and Propriety "say, *But he hath not given me over unto* "*Death.* We can truly say, that he hath "not dealt with us after our Sins, nor re‑ "warded us according to our Iniquities; "that he hath corrected us but not in his "Anger, since in the Midst of Judgment "he remember'd Mercy. Though the "Flames were fierce and dreadful yet he "did not overthrow us, as he did the Ci‑ "ties of *Sodom* and *Gomorrah*, nor make "us a standing Memorial of his Wrath to "all succeeding Ages; but as a most ten‑ "der and compassionate Father, he had "Mercy on us, and as soon as he saw "our Adversity he was moved to pity "and commiserate our Distress. Many "were the Hearts and Hands that he "then opened; many and gracious were "the refreshing Showers that he then "poured down upon our Heads; and "by the speedy and liberal Contributions "that were then raised, were the imme‑ "diate and urgent Necessities of many "poor Sufferers supplied, and they in a "Measure preserved from Hunger, Cold, "and Nakedness; Evils, which after so "deplorable a Calamity seem'd almost
"unavoid‑

"unavoidable Persons of the highest
"Rank, and in the most eminent Stati-
"ons, did not think it beneath their
"Dignity to take pity on us, to bestow
"to the Relief of our Necessities out of
"their Abundance; and by their Exam-
"ple, Authority, and Interest, to excite
"and promote the like generous Dispo-
"sition in others. And what greater
"Comfort and Consolation under so sore
"a Calamity could we wish for or desire,
"than to have our present most gracious
"Sovereign, his illustrious Consort [and
"his Highness the Prince of *Wales*]
"touched with a lively Sense of our Mise-
"ries and Misfortunes, and their Hearts
"overflowing in Streams of Pity and
"Compassion, of Bounty and Liberality
"towards us; thereby satisfying the
"empty Soul, and filling the hungry Soul
"with Goodness; and in their Persons
"verifying what the Prophet *Isaiah* had
"long before uttered concerning the
"Church in its most flourishing Estate,
"*Kings shall be thy Nursing Fathers, and*
"*Queens thy Nursing Mothers* [m]."

[m] *His present Majesty gave to the poor Sufferers* 1000 l. *the Queen* 200 l. *the Prince of* Wales 100 l. *to be distributed by the Direction of the Honourable* George Do=
dington.

But

But to come to a *Conclusion* of this *sad Story*; if after such *severe Strokes* of the *Divine Displeasure* which we have felt, and after such *eminent Appearances* of the *Divine Goodness* on our Behalf, we should trespass yet more against the Lord, will not the following Mark of *Infamy* be justly set upon us, THIS IS THAT BLANDFORD! To prevent which ignominious Brand, give me leave to subjoin some serious Considerations upon the Subject of Divine *Providence*; which, with the *Address* that follows, may, through the *Divine Blessing*, be of Service to us all, if conscientiously improved by us.

N.B. *Many other* Particulars, *remarkable* and *affecting*, to those especially who were more *immediately* concern'd in them, might have been inserted here also; but I have found my self under a *Necessity* not only to *omit them*, but considerably to *contract* what I had *at first* thrown together, both in the *foregoing History* and the *following Address*, that the *Price* may be easy to every *Buyer*.

A SERMON

PREACHED AT

BLANDFORD,

JUNE the 4th. 1735.

PSAL. cxix. 91.

----- *All are thy Servants.*

HE Doctrine of a *Providence* is so reasonable and comfortable a Notion, that no one can well forbear giving in to the Belief of it, or even wishing it to be true; no one would choose to have it otherwise, but those whose Consciences

tell

tell them, they have by their Sins justly forfeited its Care. Such may well dread the *almighty Governor* of the World, who can make, if he sees fitting, the meanest of his Creatures, or the most useful, Instruments of their Ruin.

No wonder that the *Epicureans* denied a Providence, who ridiculously imagined the World was formed by *Chance*. Could we *believe* the *one* we might consistently *deny* the *other*. Whereas " Confusion (as " one observes) is the Effect of *Chance*, " but *Order* the Product of *Art* and Indu-" stry." Now Order and Harmony are so evident in all the Parts of the Universe, that they clearly point out a *designing, governing Cause*. Which Way soever we turn our Eyes, or employ our Thoughts, we may trace the Footsteps of *Divine Wisdom* in the amazing Formation of Things, in their admirable Dependance one upon another, and in their general and known Usefulness. If we look to the *Heavens above*, the glorious Luminaries there, together with their steady and constant Revolutions, and benign Influences upon us, plainly bespeak the consummate Wisdom and Skill of the great Architect. If we traverse the *Earth* on which we live, and take a View of the various Animals and Vegetables in their surprizing and beautiful Formation, Preservation, and Successions, these all proclaim aloud their wise and great Author, and his superintending Providence. Yea, when we dig into the Bowels of the Earth, such useful Materials are produced from thence, as bring with them new Proofs of the Doctrine here asserted. Again, if we descend into the *Deep*, the Sea, with the Things that are therein, together with its constant Flux and Reflux, declare the Glory of God, his handy Work, and his commanding Influence. In short, who is there, but will, upon a mature Consideration of Things, find himself under a kind of Necessity (if he will follow the Dictates of right Reason) of rejecting the absurd Notion of an accidental World, and of confessing, that by a wise and omnipotent God all Things were made, and that by *him all Things consist*.

" He that tells me (says Archbishop
" *Tillotson* in his sixth Vol. *p.* 237.) that
" this great and curious Frame of the
" World was made by Chance, I could
" much more believe him, if he should
" tell me that *Henry* the Seventh's Chapel,
" in *Westminster*, was not built by any
" mortal Man, but the Stones did grow
" in those Forms into which they seem
" to us to be cut and graven; the Stones,
" and

"and Timber, and Iron, and Brass, and
"all the other Materials, came thither by
"Chance, and upon a Day met all happi-
"ly together, and put themselves into
"that delicate Order in which we see
"them so close compacted, that it must
"be a great Chance that parts them again.
"Now is it not much easier to imagine
"how a skilful Workman should raise a
"Building, than how Timber and Stones,
"and how that Variety of Materials,
"which is required to a great and stately
"Building, should meet together all of a
"just Bigness, and exactly fitted, and by
"Chance take their Places, and range
"themselves into that Order."

The Doctrine of *Providence* is plainly reveal'd in *Scripture*, and what every sincere Christian accounts himself vastly indebted to God for. This great Truth, so much the Comfort of all good Men, the *Psalmist* plainly asserts in the Words of my Text; *They continue this Day according to thine Ordinances For all are thy Servants*, i. e. as God *made the Earth by his Power, established the World by his Wisdom, and stretched out the Heavens by his Discretion*[n]; so they abide according to the Divine Appointment to this Day: And they not on-

---

[n] Jer. x. 12.

ly remain as a manifest and convincing Proof of the Being of God, and as a signal Display of his glorious Perfections in their first most beautiful and harmonious Formation, but they continue this Day according to his Ordinances, that he may use and employ them to fulfil the wise and righteous Purposes of his *providential Government*, in the several Ages of the World, *For all are his Servants, all are his Servants*, i.e. the Heaven, the Earth, and the Seas, the Sun, the Moon, and the Stars; the Earth with all that is thereon, and whatsoever *passeth through the Paths of the Seas*, are obedient to the sovereign Will of their great Lord and Creator: O God! thou art the absolute and sole Lord of the Universe; who is a God like unto thee! All thy Creatures from the highest to the lowest, from the greatest to the meanest, whether rational or irrational, whether animate or inanimate, shall obey thy Voice, *Ut servi Heris*, as Servants their Masters, *For all are thy Servants; obediunt & adsunt tibi ad nutum* [o]; a Word, a Look, a Nod of thine will make them all swift to fulfil thy Pleasure.

[o] Pool's Synop. Critic.

Now that I may the better answer the Design of this Day, I shall shew,

I. That the Divine Providence extends to all Parts of the Creation
II. That the several Parts of the Creation, as under his Direction, shall subserve his Will and Pleasure.
III. How, or in what Manner the Providence of God makes use of them to accomplish his Will. And,
IV. What we may reasonably suppose to be some of the special Intentions of Providence under any uncommon Events, relating to larger or lesser Societies of Men, or to particular Persons. Of these in their Order.

I. *That the Divine Providence extends to all Parts of the Creation.*

There is nothing but what comes under his Cognizance and Care. He is every Way able to govern the World without any Difficulty, yea, with all possible Ease. None can controul him, or say, what dost thou? *He doth whatsoever he pleaseth in the Army of Heaven, and among the Inhabitants of the Earth*[p]. His Ability is manifest from his infinite Knowledge, Wisdom,

[p] Dan. iv. 25.

Power, Patience and Immensity From whence we may infer the *Certainty* of his *universal* Providence, especially, when we consider his overflowing Goodness, together with the near Relation he stands in to the whole as the Creator of the World *All Things were made by him* [q] *We are all the Work of his Hands; we are his Off-spring* [r]. The Unconcernedness of the Ostrich for her young Ones is mentioned as unnatural and cruel, *She is harden'd against her young Ones, as though they were not hers* [s]. Nothing renders a Man, especially a Christian, more infamous, than to be without *natural Affection* [t], than not to *provide for his own* [u]. If any Thing of this Nature be an Imperfection in an irrational Creature, and a gross Crime in a rational Creature, surely then every Thing of this Kind must be at an infinite Remove from the great Parent of all Beings, in whom dwells every Perfection.

It was owing to their Ignorance of God, that the Heathens imagined the lesser Things of Life were not the Concern of Heaven. *Magna curant Dii, parva negligunt*, Cicero. But God knows all Things, fills all Things; is every where present

[q] John i. 3. [r] Acts xvii. 28. [s] Job xxxix. 16.
[t] 2 Tim. iii. 3. [u] 1 Tim v 8.

with

with all Things, and doubtless takes care of, guides and governs all Things. *Am I a God at Hand, saith the Lord, and not a God afar off? Can any hide himself in secret Places, that I shall not see him, saith the Lord! Do not I fill Heaven and Earth, saith the Lord*[x]*!*

As the *Providence* of God extends to the noblest Angel in the highest Heaven, *Angels, Authorities, and Powers, are subject unto him*[y]; so also to the most insignificant Creature in this World *Are not two Sparrows sold for a Farthing? And one of them shall not fall on the Ground without your Father But the very Hairs of your Head are all numbered*[z].

The civth *Psalm* throughout is a most admirable Description of the extensive Providence of God. There we find that the Heaven, the Earth and Seas, and all Things that are in them, as they had their Existence from him, so they have their absolute Dependance on him *These wait all upon thee, that thou mayest give them their Meat in due Season. That thou givest them they gather,* &c. —— *Thou takest away their Breath, they die,* —— ver. 27, 28. And if the Providence of God extends to the more ignoble

[x] Jer. xxiii. 23, 24. [y] 1 Pet. iii. 22. [z] Matt. x. 29, 30.

Parts

Parts of the Creation, to the Birds of the Air, to the Beasts of the Field, and to the *Lillies that grow there* [a]; much more to his rational and superior Creatures, and more especially unto good Men, who are a Part of *his own Family, his Children* The *Eyes of the Lord run to and fro throughout the whole Earth, to shew himself strong in the Behalf of them whose Heart is perfect towards him* [b]. And if we are by Christ's Order to be peculiarly benevolent to his Disciples, *As we have Opportunity let us do good unto all Men, especially unto them who are of the Houshold of Faith* [c]; how much more will our Lord himself have his *little Flock* under his peculiar Care. Yea, his particular Concern for these is urged as an Argument against the ill Treatment of any, even the least of them *Take heed therefore that ye despise not one of these little Ones; for I say unto you, that in Heaven their Angels do always behold the Face of my Father which is in Heaven* [d]; who as Ministers of Divine Providence stand ready to receive and execute their Commission from God, to avenge the ill Usage his Children meet with from Men. Sinners, were they wise, would for their own sake, dread being unkind

[a] Matt. vi. 28, 30.   [b] 2 Chron. xvi 9.   [c] Gal. vi 10.   [d] Matt. xviii 10.

and cruel to any of the Servants of the most high God, whose Concern for them will procure his Resentment against their merciless Enemies.

As the Divine Providence extends to all Parts of the Creation, so

> II. *These several Parts of the Creation, as under God's Direction, have, and shall subserve his Will and Pleasure. — For all are thy Servants.*

Here I could produce a great Variety of Instances to shew, that the *rational, irrational*, and *inanimate* Parts of the Creation, are all made use of as Instruments to accomplish the Divine Purposes in the Government of the World.

To begin with the most excellent. The glorious Inhabitants of Heaven, the Angels of God have been imployed by him for this end: Thus they went and comforted *Jacob* in his lonely and distressed Condition[e]. So an angelic Host encompassed and secured *Elisha* and his Servant, when they struck their Enemies with Blindness, and delivered them over to their Will[f]. The Angel of the Lord smote the Camp of the *Assyrians* at his Command,

[e] Gen. xxviii. 12. [f] 2 Kings vi. 17, 18.

even *an hundred fourscore and five Thousand: Are they not all ministring Spirits, sent forth to minister for them who shall be Heirs of Salvation*[g]? *They do his Commandments, hearkening to the Voice of his Word. They do his Pleasure*[i].

The once exalted, but now most abandoned Part of the Creation, even *apostate Spirits*, are forced to quit those whom they possessed, when the Lord of all has Purposes to serve thereby worthy of himself.

Good Men, under the Divine Influences, are persuaded to do their best to fulfil God's Word; and *bad Men*, though against their Inclinations and Design, are so over-ruled, as to help forward the Counsels of the Almighty. *O Assyrian, the Rod of mine Anger, and the Staff in their Hand is mine Indignation. Howbeit, he meaneth not so, neither doth his Heart think so*[k].

The *animate irrational* Parts of the Creation, even the Birds and Beasts of Prey, have been, and are at hand to serve the Purposes of his Providence, either to preserve his Servants, or punish his Enemies. Thus at God's Command the Ra-

[g] 2 Kings xix. 35. Isai. xxxvii. 36. [h] Heb. i. 14. [i] Psal. ciii. 20, 21. [k] Isai. x. 7.

vens [1] shall feed the Prophet *Elijah* [m]: The Lions shall fawn on *Daniel* whilst they instantly devour his Accusers [n]. In the Time of *Egypt*'s Plagues what Swarms of Insects infest their Land at his sovereign Word! *He spake, and there came divers sorts of Flies, and Lice in all their Coasts. He spake and the Locusts came, and Caterpillars, and that without Number* [o]. If God pleases, by the Worms we tread under our Feet, *the lofty Looks of Men shall be humbled, and the Haughtiness of Men,* yea, of Kings, *shall be brought down,* even to the Dust. *And immediately the Angel of the Lord smote* Herod, *because he gave not God the Glory: And he was eaten of Worms and gave up the Ghost* [p].

The inanimate Parts of God's Creation also have, and shall serve the Purposes of their absolute Lord; *For all are his Servants.* Thus the heavenly Luminaries, though they ordinarily obey the standing Laws of their great Maker, and keep their wonted Courses, yet if the fulfilling his Will demands it, and a new Law be

---

[1] *Or,* if by Ravens we are to understand some of the human Race, as some will have it, yet it was owing to the same interposing Hand of God that they were so kind and benevolent to his Servant *Elijah*

[m] 1 Kings xvii. 4, 6. [n] Dan. vi. 22, 24. [o] Psal. cv. 31, 34. [p] Acts xii. 23.

issued forth from the Throne of Heaven they instantly obey it, and cease their Motion. *Sun, stand thou still upon Gibeon, and thou Moon in the Valley of Ajalon. And the Sun stood still, and the Moon stayed* [q] *The Stars*, at God's bidding, *in their Courses fought against Sisera* [r] *He has his Treasures of the Snow, and Treasures of the Hail, which he hath reserved against the Time of Trouble, against the Day of Battle and War* [s]. Thus we read, that *the Lord cast down great Hailstones from Heaven upon them*, viz. the Amorites, *unto Azekah, and they died* [t]. Storms and Tempests shall rise high, and rage vehemently, or hush into Silence, at a Word of Command from him. *He gathereth the Wind in his Fists* [u]. Thus our Lord *rebuked the Wind, and said unto the Sea, Peace, be still And the Wind ceased, and there was a great Calm* [x]. Fire and Water become raging and destructive, if such be their Commission from the eternal God. These, as we commonly observe, are good Servants, but bad Masters; and yet even then, when they grow too powerful for our Restraint, and bear down all before them, they are God's Servants, and accomplish his righteous Purposes. By the

[q] Josh. x. 12, 13. [r] Judges v. 20. [s] Job xxxvii. 22, 23. [t] Josh. x. 11. [u] Prov. xxx. 4. [x] Mark iv. 39.

Blandford, June 4. 1735.

one and by the *other*, God has destroyed both Persons and Places: *And there came down Fire from Heaven and destroyed Ahaziah's Captain and his fifty*[y]. By an Inundation [z] of the River *Kishon* the Enemies of God's *Israel* were destroyed *The River* Kishon *swept them away, that ancient River, the River* Kishon [a]. As by the one God delug'd the old World, so by the other the present shall be consumed: *The Elements shall melt with fervent Heat; the Earth also, and the Works that are therein, shall be burnt up* [b].

What Folly then, to make this God our Enemy, who can arm the whole Creation against us; and can make that which we daily use and need, to be the Instrument of our Destruction! Nay, *who after he hath killed has Power to cast into Hell* [c]!

[y] 2 Kings i. 10.
[z] Though we have felt the dreadful Effects of raging Flames, yet our Grief was not renewed, nor were we render'd inconsolable by a late unusual Inundation, as was a few Months past mentioned in a publick Paper, that Account was utterly false. Indeed we deserve new Marks of his Displeasure, but blessed be God, *he is Long-suffering to us ward, not willing that any should perish, but that all should come to Repentance,* 2 Pet. iii. 9.
[a] Judges v. 21. [b] 2 Pet. iii. 10. [c] Luke xii. 5.

What Wisdom to secure his Favour! An omnipotent Friend is most valuable. The true Christian is an happy Man. The God of Heaven and Earth is his Covenant God. The very Calamities he now shares in with others shall prove to him merciful Dispensations. *Our light Affliction*, says the Apostle, *which is but for a Moment, worketh for us a far more exceeding and an eternal Weight of Glory.* May the obtaining his Love and Favour be the Matter of our daily fervent Prayer, and be esteemed by us the grand Concern of Life. But to shew,

III. *How, or in what Manner the blessed God, in his Providence, makes use of the several Parts of the Creation to subserve his Pleasure.*

Most certain it is, that *God's Ways are in the Dark, and his Footsteps are not known.* We cannot enter into his Secrets, nor is it fit we should. *Who will say unto him, what dost thou*[d]? Yet thus much we may conclude, that he disposes and manages all Things in Heaven and Earth, in order to answer the Ends of his Government, in a Way suitable to *his own* Nature, and agreeable to the Nature of his Creatures.

[d] Job ix. 12.

1st In a Way suitable to *his own* Nature.

Though none can controul or prevent him from fulfilling his Counsels; yet we may be sure that he always acts agreeable to his own most perfect Rectitude. When we cannot perceive the Footsteps of Wisdom and Mercy; nay, can discern little else than the Marks of Anger and dreadful Displeasure, and thereupon may be ready to arraign his very Justice, yet we may be confident of this, that his Works are perfect, conformable to infinite Wisdom, Justice, Compassion and Love. He is still *wise in Heart; just and right is he* [e]. Yea, *All the Paths of the Lord are Mercy and Truth, unto such as keep his Covenant and his Testimonies* [f].

2dly. In a Way agreeable to the Nature of the several Parts of his *Creation*.

Here *some* may be considered as under his more *absolute* Sway, having no rational Powers to conduct or determine themselves. *Others* there are, who being indued with rational Powers, are capable of moral Government, and in the Divine Management and Disposal of Things are considered as such, without supposing any such Influences or Impressions as would

[e] Deut. xxxii. 4.   [f] Psal. xxv. 10.

necessitate any of their Actions However, he can and will over-rule all their Intentions, Counsels and Actions, so as to promote and accomplish the wise, righteous, and kind Purposes of his Providence by them. His Methods are too deep for us in many Things to fathom. Yet as something of the Mind and Will of God in his Dispensations is made known to us in *Revelation*, this is what we may and ought diligently to inquire after. Which brings us to consider,

IV. *What we may reasonably suppose to be some of the special Intentions of Providence under any unusual or uncommon Events, relating to larger or lesser Societies, or to particular Persons.*

Unusual, and most awful Events, however effected, whether by the more immediate Hand of God, or by the Instrumentality of his Creatures, whether the most exalted or the meanest of them, as they fulfil the Mind and Will of God, *For all are his Servants*; so they have their Meaning, their Language to us also: And so far as God's providential Dispensations bear a Relation to his *Kingdom of Grace*, particularly as to the erecting or establishing of it in our Hearts, so far we are immediately concerned our selves; and not notwithstanding the many knotty Intricacies that attend his Proceedings in other respects, for as the Prophet speaks, *Verily thou art a God that hidest thy self* [g]; we yet may humbly desire to know the Meaning of them, so far as this Knowledge may help us the better to *understand* our Duty, or to *discharge* it. This was the Concern of pious *Job*. *I will say unto God, do not condemn me, shew me wherefore thou contendest with me* [h]. Though it would be daring Presumption to desire to know of God, what were his particular *Reasons*, as the great *Governor* of the World, for laying in Ashes almost a whole Town; or why *this* and *that*, and not some *other*; yet he will not take it ill at our Hands, if we, having his Glory and our spiritual Advantage at heart, employ our Minds agreeable to his Word and Will, in searching into the Causes of his severe Dispensations towards us; nay, a total Neglect here would be very criminal and dangerous. *Because they regard not the Works of the Lord, nor the Operation of his Hands, he shall destroy them, and not build them up.*

Now the *Providences* of God may be either of a prosperous or an *afflictive* Kind.

[g] Isai. xlv. 15.   [h] Job x. 2.

The

The Occasion of our assembling together on this Day inclines me at present to treat only of the latter.

When the Events of Providence are very severe and afflictive, no one can question but that God intends some weighty and useful Instruction by them. And it becomes us diligently to enquire what this is. And,

1. God's ordinary Design in such awakening Dispensations is to correct and punish Persons for their Sins.

Though it does not follow, because we have been greater *Sufferers* than others, that therefore we are greater *Sinners*; yet, had we not been *Sinners* we had not been *Sufferers*. Had we not provoked the Lord to Anger by our Iniquities, we had not been in such desolating and low Circumstances as we lately were, and as some yet are. Thus the Prophet speaks, *Your Iniquities have turned away these Things, and your Sins have with-holden good Things from you* [i]. As *Affliction cometh not forth of the Dust, neither doth Trouble spring out of the Ground* [k]; so the bitter Root they spring from we are told is Sin. *Shall I not visit for these Things, saith the Lord! Shall not my Soul be avenged on such a People as this* [l]*! Fools, because*

[i] Jer. v. 25. [k] Job v. 6. [l] Jer. v. 29.

of their Transgressions, and because of their Iniquities, are afflicted [m]. Our Sins, our Iniquities doubtless, procured our Distresses. O Israel! O Blandford! *thou hast destroyed thy self.* When we behold Towns and Villages laid waste and desolate, tho' we ought not hastily to conclude they were Sinners more than others, yet we should always conclude, that *Sin lieth at the Door.* If any think otherwise, it is owing to their wretched Stupidity, and gross Ignorance of the Nature of Sin, the Nature of God, or the Contents of the Bible. Would to God, we were more deeply sensible of our Sins, the God-provoking Cause of our Ruin; and that we could more feelingly say, *Rivers of Waters run down our Eyes because we have not kept thy Law* [n]!

2. We may reasonably suppose, that another Thing God intends by such awful and alarming Providences, is to convince Men more fully of the Uncertainty and Insufficiency of earthly Enjoyments.

Experience plainly tells us, how prone we are to set our Hearts inordinately on the *Things that are seen.* We are too apt, *in our Prosperity,* to think, if not to say, *we shall never be moved* [o]. And under this

---

[m] Psal. cvii. 17. [n] Psal. cxix. 136. [o] Psal. xxx. 6.

vain Conceit we suffer our Affections to take too fast hold of Things that are fleeting and perishing. So that a wise and good God sees it sometimes necessary to correct us in such a Manner, that we may learn by his *Rod*, what we *might* and *ought* to have learnt by his Word, *viz. Vanity of Vanity, all is Vanity* [p]; and, *That Man at his best Estate is altogether Vanity* [q]. One Hour he is in flourishing Circumstances, ready to say, *Soul, thou hast much Goods laid up for many Years; take thine Ease, eat, drink, and be merry* [r]. The next, perhaps, he hath not enough left to satisfy the Cravings of Nature, or to furnish him with the Necessaries of Life. Ah! Who would set their Hearts on that *which is not?* which is but a little Remove from nothing, even when in our swelling, though vain Imagination, it appears to be substantial Riches. Seeing then we have had such a flagrant, and one would hope convincing Proof of the Instability and Emptiness of all earthly Comforts, let us from hence learn to *rejoice as if we rejoiced not, to weep as though we wept not, to buy as tho' we possessed not; for the Fashion of this World passeth away.*

[p] Eccles. i. 1. [q] Psal. xxxix. 5. [r] Luke xii. 29.

3. By

3 By such calamitous Events God may design to try the *Charity* of Men; and this both as it is *opposed* to *Censure* and rash *Judgment*, and as it *includes Liberality* and *Beneficence.*

(1) As it is opposed to *Censure* and *rash Judgment.*

Though God afflicts Persons, Families or Places, and that in an unusual Way, yet we must not for this Reason *only* infer, that they are marked out by Heaven for Sinners *above all others*, lest we offend God, and add Affliction to the afflicted by such uncharitable Surmises; yet when Men shall commit Crimes so infamous, as well as notorious, that these loudly proclaim the Cause of their Sufferings; as in the Case of *Sodom*; or when some remarkable and signal Calamities shall overtake *known* merciless, and cruel Persecutors, in their hellish and bloody Pursuits; in such Instances, it would be no breach of Charity to say, that God made them *Examples* of Terror to those that *after should live ungodly.* But then in other Cases our Charity should prompt us to put a milder Interpretation upon God's Dealings with Men, and incline us to pronounce them rather *corrective* than *judicial* This was the Doctrine our Saviour taught, when he was on Earth, to prevent or cure this

cen-

censorious Temper, and to let us see we cannot be blameless if we indulge it. *There were present at that Season some that told him of the* Galileans, *whose Blood* Pilate *had mingled with their Sacrifices. And Jesus answering, said unto them, Suppose ye that these* Galileans *were Sinners above all the* Galileans, *because they suffered such Things? I tell you nay. Or those Eighteen upon whom the Tower in* Siloam *fell, and slew them, think ye they were Sinners above all Men that dwelt in* Jerusalem? *I tell you nay* [s].

Let Persons that are remarkably chastened of the Lord be as severe as they will in judging *themselves*, few are in danger of exceeding here. But let *others*, out of *Pity* to the Afflicted, and from a Sense of their own Frailty and Miscarriages, be more modest; *Judge not that ye be not judged* [t].

I would not be thought to intimate by this, as if I imagined, we were not *deservedly* corrected of God for our Sins; no, sure I am, that God hath *punished us less than our Iniquities deserve*; and that our Calamities, great as they are, don't call us to suitable Repentance and Humiliation. But I would not have other Towns or Places think they are so far *inferior* to us in

---

[s] Luke xiii. 1, 6.   [t] Matth. vii. 1.

Wicked-

Wickedness as to be themselves out of *danger.* Our blessed Saviour intended to rouse in Men very different Thoughts and Apprehensions in the Place just now named. *I tell you nay; but except ye repent, ye shall likewise perish.* But more to this Purpose will be mentioned in a following Particular.

(2.) As it includes *Liberality* and *Beneficence.*

The *Miseries* of *some* are intended by Providence as an Opportunity to prove the *Charity* of *others*; in *extraordinary Calamities,* by their *extraordinary Supplies.* Such were our Calamities, and such has been the Liberality of our Fellow-Christians. Our *great Trial of Affliction abounded unto the Riches of others Liberality; for to their Power, yea, some beyond their Power* [u], *were willing of themselves,* desiring those who took upon them the kind Office of collecting others Charity to receive their Gifts. This Forwardness was discover'd in many Places. *Thanks be unto God for his unspeakable Gifts* [x], and to Men we owe the most grateful Returns.

4. By the awful and severe *Trials* of *some*, God intends a *Warning* to *others.*

[u] 2 Cor. viii. 2, 3, 4.   [x] 2 Cor. ix. 15.

So kind is the blessed God in his Nature, so merciful in his Intentions, that when maintaining the Honour of his violated most righteous Laws, requires him to punish *some*, he hereby intends also to give *Warning* unto *others*, this the Apostle asserts when he says, that *with many of the Israelites God was not well pleased; for they were overthrown in the Wilderness. Now these Things were our Examples, to the Intent we should not lust after evil Things as they also lusted. Neither be ye Idolaters, as were some of them. Neither let us commit Fornication, as some of them committed, and fell in one Day three and twenty Thousand. Neither let us tempt Christ, as some of them also tempted, and were destroyed of Serpents. Neither murmur ye, as some of them also murmured, and were destroyed of the Destroyer. Now all these Things hapned unto them for Ensamples. And they are written for our Admonition, upon whom the Ends of the World are come. Wherefore let him that thinketh he standeth take heed lest he fall* y.

A jealous, just, and gracious God, would have those that are in prosperous Circumstances to observe the Calamities of others; that they may avoid every Thing that has the least Tendency to displease

---

y 1 Cor. x. 5——12.

… and provoke him; do every Thing to obtain his Favour, yea, so observe his Dealings with others, that they may be prepared for whatever Distresses may overtake them. May every one learn from God's heavy Hand upon us, and we much more, not to offend him who hath made us to drink of the Cup of his Wrath.

5. Another Design in such Providences is to teach us the better to *commiserate others* in their calamitous Circumstances.

A Tenderness of Spirit is such a charitable Temper of Mind that 'tis worth gaining, though it be by our enduring sharp Afflictions. The Treasures of the Mind are vastly preferable to all the unsatisfactory and perishing Riches of the World. We hereby more resemble the God of Love; who *in all our Afflictions is afflicted*[z]; who is *full of Compassion and gracious*[a].

We have found the Need of others most compassionate Regards for us; and should have thought it hard to have wanted their Pity, their Help, and their Prayers. *Their Abundance* has been a kind *Supply to our Wants*[b]. May their Favours bestowed on us, so liberal, and so seasonable, be-

[z] Isa. lxiii. 9. [a] Psal. lxxxvi. 15. [b] 2 Cor. viii. 14

get and establish in us a tender and benevolent Temper towards others. Should any of our late bounteous Friends, or others, be in sad Distress (from which God preserve them) and we hereafter able to help them, it would argue Hearts harder than Rocks, should we not be thus disposed. Or should we want *Ability*, a *Tenderness* towards them in their Distresses is such a Temper which Persons so afflicted as we have been, should carefully cherish. Every Thing of Hardness and Severity towards others, in us, must be peculiarly aggravated, considering what melting, softning Providences we have been under. It was said by God of old Time, *Thou shalt neither vex a Stranger, nor oppress him* [c]. And if not a Stranger, much less one of the same Nation or Place, or one that has been a Fellow-Sufferer with our selves; *For ye were Strangers in the Land of* Egypt. And again, *Thou shalt not oppress a Stranger. For ye know the Heart of a Stranger, seeing ye were Strangers in the Land of* Egypt [d].

All afflictive Providences, as they should prove a Means of encreasing our *Faith* and *Patience*, so of begetting in us more of that Christian *Meekness* and *Fellow-feeling*, which

[c] Exod. xxii. 21.   [d] Exod. xxiii. 9.

would be very ornamental to our Profession. We should hereby learn to *put on Bowels of Mercies*ᵉ, and to *weep with those that weep*ᶠ.

6. We may reasonably suppose that by such awful Providences, God further intends to mind us how much it is our *Interest* as well as *Duty*, to seek after a more durable Good; even an Inheritance *incorruptible, and that fadeth not away.*

We have *seen an End of all Perfection*ᵍ. We were situated in a pleasant and an agreeable Place; we had Houses full of good Things; we were possessed of many Comforts of Life; but alas! how soon were we stript of all! And what is the Inference we should draw from hence? What Use does God expect we should make of it? Nothing less than this surely, (which God grant) that seeing our late *earthly Houses*, literally speaking, were so suddenly and surprizingly laid in Ruin, that we make sure of an unalienable Claim to a *Building of God, Houses not made with Hands, eternal in the Heavens*ʰ.

And as we were thus unexpectedly turned out of our Habitations by the great Lord of all, so many other good Things

ᵉ Col iii. 12.   ᶠ Rom. xii. 15.   ᵍ Psal. cxix. 96.
ʰ 2 Cor. v. 1.

also, which we were loath to part with, were quickly and irresistibly snatched from us; how highly reasonable then is it, that we learn from hence to lay up our main Stock, our *Treasures in Heaven*, where they will be for ever safe and secure from the Reach of all wasting and destructive Accidents. There no Thief can approach nor Flames devour and waste.

7. Another Design of such melancholy Providences may be, more fully to satisfy us of the solid Supports, and real Pleasures, which Religion affords us.

Many faithful Servants of God have found the sweetest Comfort in the most afflicted Parts of Life. As their Afflictions have abounded, so has their Consolation also When the blessed God has by some severe Providences convinced them of the Emptiness of earthly Enjoyments, then has it pleased him to fill them with *Joy and Peace in believing*[1]. When the World has failed them their God has not, but has been a present Help in Trouble. When the *Streams* have been cut off they have been more readily inclined to seek to the *Fountain*, and thence have drawn Waters of Refreshment. *Knowing in themselves that they have in Heaven a better and*

---

[1] Rom. xv. 13.

endu-

enduring Substance [k]; they have taken the more patiently, yea, *joyfully the spoiling of their Goods*. And seeing it was the Lord of all that did it, whose Right cannot be disputed, and *their* Lord, who, as he is Head of the Universe, so also *Head over all Things* for the Good of his *Church* [l], and who chastens whom he loves, they will neither resist his Will nor suspect his Love. What was the Language of the holy Psalmist? *It is good for me that I have been afflicted, that I might learn thy Statutes:* And then adds his Reasons for it, *the Law of thy Mouth is better unto me than Thousands of Gold and Silver* [m].

The Testimony of a good Conscience, the Hopes of the Divine Favour, through the Merits and Mediation of our Lord Jesus Christ; the Witness of God's Holy Spirit; the believing Views of a glorious World, have *yielded* to many the most *reviving Comfort*, even when under the most depressing worldly Calamities. This the pious *Psalmist* knew, and therefore prayed, *When my Heart is overwhelmed, lead me to the Rock that is higher than I* [n]. Happy Soul! that can say in the Words of the Prophet, *Although the Fig-Tree shall not blos-*

[k] Heb. x. 34. [l] Eph. i. 22. [m] Psal. cxix. 71, 72. [n] Psal. lxi. 2.

som,

som, neither Fruit be in the Vine, and the Fields shall yield no Meat, &c. yet I will rejoice in the Lord, I will joy in the God of my Salvation º.

8. and *Lastly*, God by such sad and awful Events may intend to *quicken* us in our *Preparations* for a better World.

Seeing after all our utmost Pains and Labour in gathering together the good Things of this Life, and pleasing our selves with the Hope of a long Enjoyment of them, these may by some unexpected, and sad Turn of Providence, be suddenly snatched from us, what is the Use that every one of us should make of it? Learn hence, O my Soul, seeing *here is no continuing City, to seek one to come* ᴾ. Lord help me, by the *powerful Influences* of thy Holy Spirit, to be more diligent than ever in using aright every Talent; in improving precious Time; in getting some Good from every Occurrence of Providence; in seeking for Strength and Comfort from every Ordinance; that hereby thou mayst be help'd on with more Speed and Pleasure in thy Way to that better World above, where *there remains a Rest to the People of God* ᑫ. Here's nothing I can long call my own; above there are Riches that

º Hab. iii. 17, 18. ᴾ Heb. xiii. 14. ᑫ Heb. iv. 9.

can never be lost; a Building that can never be destroyed; an *Inheritance undefiled and eternal; living Fountains of Joy; Pleasures for evermore; a Crown of Glory that fadeth not away*[r]; *a City that hath Foundations, whose Builder and Maker is God*[s]. There dwells my Saviour, my God. Would to God, that I, and others also, may be so happy as to make Choice of these for our Portion and everlasting All.

When once by Divine Grace we are become so wise and happy, as to make these our Choice, and are made *meet for the Inheritance of the Saints in Light,* then we shall have nothing very sad to fear, whilst we remain in this gloomy World, seeing nothing very sad can befal us that can touch our main Interest. All that remains to make us as happy as we can be at present, is to be daily providing for the Heavenly State, to have our Claim to the *promised Inheritance,* the Purchase of our dear Redeemer's precious Blood, cleared up; then may we stretch forth our most eager Desires after the full Possession, impatiently longing to take our Leave of this disappointing and sinful World, that we may go and be with Jesus. Then may we rejoice in the *Hopes of the*

[r] 1 Pet. v. 4.   [s] Heb. xi. 10.

Glory of God, being fully assured, that in our *Father's House are many Mansions*[t], and that our blessed Saviour is gone *to prepare a Place for us*. In the firm Belief, and pleasing Expectation of which may we spend our few remaining Days, *Looking for that blessed Hope, and the glorious Appearing of the great God and our Saviour Jesus Christ*[u], when he will receive us to himself, that *where he is we may be also*.

Now *unto him that loved us, and washed us from our Sins in his own Blood; and hath made us Kings and Priests unto God and his Father, to him be Glory and Dominion for ever and ever*[x]. Amen.

[t] John xiv. 2, 3, 4.   [u] Tit. ii. 13.   [x] Rev. 1. 5, 6.

AN ADDRESS TO THE INHABITANTS OF *BLANDFORD*.

THE melancholy and shocking Events of *that dreadful Day*, when Providence laid us in Ashes, have been, as I have often observed, the grand Topick of Conversation. My Design in the following Pages is not to please *Men* but *God*, who searcheth the Hearts. Bear with me therefore in dealing plainly with you. I hope I shall offend *none* though I take the Liberty of applying to *all*. The *Almighty God* hath spoken so loudly

loudly to us that one cannot easily keep silence; *The Lion hath roared, who will not fear? The Lord hath spoken, who can but prophecy*[a]?

I persuade my self, that none are utterly insensible of the Hand of God, and that all have made some just Reflections on such an *awful Event*. I hope it has been the Language of every one's Heart, God hath done right but we have done wickedly. Such an Apprehension is *proper*, but not *sufficient*. We shall make very little of our great Distress, unless we descend to a more particular Consideration of our selves under it. *Guilt*, like *Calamities*, will affect us most when personally considered. The nearer we perceive our selves concerned in the *one*, or the *other*, the deeper will be the Impression. In the *one* Case we are soon sensibly affected, I mean as to our personal Losses and Sufferings; would to God we were more feelingly affected with the *other*, each one with his *own* Sins. A *confused Apprehension*, and *general Acknowledgment* of Guilt, will not produce such valuable and lasting Fruits as both God and Man may justly expect from us. There never will be, there never can be, a real Repentance, till it becomes *personal*; till

---

[a] Amos iii. 8.

we are each of us sensible of *our own Transgressions*. Thus the Psalmist, *I acknowledge my Transgressions, and my Sin is ever before me* [b]. That we may be so wise and happy, we must not only search and try our Ways, but conscientiously follow the Example of pious *David, Search me, O God, and know my Heart, try me, and know my Thoughts, and see if there be any wicked Way in me, and lead me in the Way everlasting* [c]. And being thus by the Holy Spirit convinced of our *own* Sins, we shall hereby be the better disposed to confess and bewail our *Family* Sins, and the Sins of *others* also. And as there are certain *Circumstances* in Affliction which have a plain and natural Tendency to bring Sin to Remembrance, and which therefore those whose Minds are rightly informed, and whose Consciences are truly tender, will be ready to observe, it becomes us to consider, whether there are not some such in our *Calamity* that may help to bring our Sins to *Remembrance*.

The *Desolation* we all know was *universal*, it touched us in every Thing almost that we valued and loved. Thus God stretched forth the Rod of his Anger, and destroyed our *Habitations*, and at the same

[b] Psal. li. 3.   [c] Psal. cxxxix. 23, 24.

G

Time also deprived us of our *worldly Substance*; the Loss both of the one, and of the other, sat heavy on our Minds, and deeply affected us. Can we forbear from hence making some such Reflections as these following: May not either our shameful Neglect of Family-Religion, or the Sins of Lewdness and Intemperance, or other Transgressions that we were chargeable with, provoke an Holy and Jealous God to say, *of a Truth many Houses shall be desolate, even once great and fair, without Inhabitant* [d]? God signified his Displeasure and Abhorrence of *Jerusalem*'s Sins by the Destruction of those *very Habitations* in which they were committed; and *they shall come and set Fire on this City, and burn it with the Houses upon whose Roofs they have offered Incense unto* Baal, *to provoke me to Anger* [e]. Again, is our Wealth wasted? How was it gained? By Oppression or Injustice? Has it not been used to maintain our Pride, to gratify our Lusts, or to indulge our Appetites? Have we employed that Share of it in those Acts of *Piety* and *Charity* which God expected, and others needed? We have suffered also severely in our *Persons. Some* you know were at once hurried into Eternity; *others* were miser-

---

[d] Isa. v. 8, 9. [e] Jer. xxxii. 29. Jer. xix. 12, 13.

ably burnt to the Hazard of their Lives; we were called to labour in the very Fire, and endured then as well as since many great Hardships and Inconveniencies We cannot err, if we ask our selves, were we not too fond of these our perishing Bodies? Too apt to indulge our Ease? Grown too secure whilst in our Prosperity? Too forgetful of God, even ready to say, *the Lord will not do Good, neither will he do Evil*[f]? Might not such a Temper as this provoke God to say, *I will punish the Men that are settled on their Lees?* — Another afflicting Circumstance of this sad Providence was this, that our public Buildings, *viz.* the *Town-Hall*, and the *Places* of our *Religious Worship*, were burnt down and destroy'd. A Circumstance that once affected us much, and may yet afford us some useful Reflections; from hence both *Magistrates* and *Ministers* may take Occasion to inquire, whether by their *Authority, Examples, Instructions,* and *Reproofs*, they duly endeavoured the Suppression of Immorality, and the Promoting *pure Religion and undefiled?* Whether they sanctified God's Sabbath themselves, and did their best towards the preventing others from profaning his *Holy Day*, whe-

[f] Zeph. i. 12.

ther by their Employments of any kind, or by other immoral Practices? Yea, it becomes every one from hence to consider, whether they have not too often sinfully *forsook the Assembling themselves together, as the Manner of some is* [g]? Or if we did attend the Places of *publick Worship*, was it with that *Seriousness, Gravity, Sincerity, Fear* and *Reverence*, as Worshippers of that God who is a *consuming Fire* [h]? Did we not too often *draw nigh unto him with our Mouth, and honour him with our Lips, when our Hearts were far from him* [i]?

Having thus mentioned some *Circumstances* of our *Calamity*, and offered my Help toward our making such Reflections as are pertinent to the present Case, that we may henceforth act that Part that becomes us as Men and Christians, and which God and Man, under such an *awakening Providence*, expects from us, and thereby render our *present Life* as agreeable as it can be, considering the uncertain Nature of Things, and the reduced and straiten'd Circumstances of many among us, and may the better provide for a *blissful Eternity*, give me leave to lay before you the *following Advice*.

[g] Heb. x. 25. [h] Heb. xii. 29. [i] Matt. xv. 8, 9.

I.

I. Let us bless God that we, and most of our dear Friends and Relatives, escaped with our *Lives*.

Some (as was before said) were cut off suddenly, and sent into an *awful Eternity*. *The Calamity*, had it been in the *Night Season*, must, in all probability, have proved fatal to *Multitudes* of us, many more would have been bewilder'd and lost in the Streets; others, in their Beds, might have slept their last, and awoke in an *eternal World*; such as were impenitent, in *quenchless Flames*. We therefore, especially such of us as were in the most imminent Danger, or that had our dear Children and Relatives most remarkably preserved, should unite in Praises to God, and say, *Bless the Lord, O our Souls, and all that is within us bless his holy Name, who redeemed our Lives from Destruction*.

II. Religiously believe that this our sore Calamity was *from God*.

Such an Apprehension of Things is pious, and, I conceive, *necessary* to the right Improvement of it: *Infidelity* in this Case will unavoidably leave Men in their old Impieties. There was hardly an *Infidel* in this Point to be found among us about *four Years* since, I hope not one *now*. We need not put this Matter on such a casual Foot as the *Philistines* did theirs with relation to the *Ark of God*, that they might know whether their Calamity was from him, or whether a *Chance* had happened to them. *Take the Ark of the Lord and send it away, that it may go. And see, if it goeth up by the Way of his own Coast to* Bethshemesh, *then he hath done this great Evil. But if not, then we shall know that it is not his Hand that smote us, it was a Chance that happen'd to us* [k]. Any Degree of Unbelief in us, who have the invaluable Privilege of a Divine Revelation, is much more culpable than in them.

Impute not our unusual Distress wholly to *second Causes*. Say not, THE FIRE could never have begun in a *worse Place*, where *four Streets* met. It could never have happen'd in a worse *Season*, when there was little *Water*, a *scorching Sun*, and a *ruffling Wind*; or when there were more *combustible Materials* (which we had provided against the approaching Winter) nor could the Wind ever have stood in a *worse Point*. All this is true, true indeed, for this was to be the *Way*, the *Time*, the *Day* of Desolation, when the *Lord said, I will not again pass by them any more* [l]. The Suddenness of it bespake the Divine Resentment, as if

---

[k] 1 Sam. vi. 8, 9. [l] Amos vii. 8.

God

God had said, I will go down and destroy them at once. So furious was the Fire, that it was more like a Torrent of Flames than a gradual Burning: Yea, the Lord *divided the Flames of Fire* [m], so that our Habitations were quickly consumed. Sudden Destruction is a Sign of God's hot Displeasure; as the Apostle observes, *Sudden Destruction shall come upon them* [n]. *Behold they shall be as Stubble. The Fire shall burn them, they shall not deliver themselves from the Power of the Flame* [o]. The *Universality* of the Desolation discovered the Divine Displeasure; the *whole* Town was soon laid in Ruins. We may here aptly apply the Words of the Prophet, *Behold the Lord maketh* this Place *empty, and maketh it waste, and turneth it upside down, and scattereth abroad the Inhabitants thereof. And it shall be, as with the People, so with the Priest, as with the Servant, so with his Master; as with the Maid, so with her Mistress; as with the Buyer, so with the Seller; as with the Lender, so with the Borrower; as with the Taker of Usury, so with the Giver of Usury to him. It shall be utterly emptied, and utterly spoiled; for the Lord hath spoken this Word* [p]. The particular *Severity* of our Affliction was another alarming Proof of God's fu-

[m] Psal. xxix. 7. [n] 1 Thess. v. 3. [o] Isa. xlvii. 14.
[p] Isa. xxiv. 1, 2, 3.

rious Rebuke; for, as has been before observed, our *Houses* were burnt, our *Substance* wasted, some were scorched to Death in the Streets, and others loaded with that afflicting Distemper, the Small-Pox; thus *Deep called unto Deep* q. And notwithstanding all those Depths of inconsolable Woe into which we were sunk, are any yet willing to impute it to meer *Chance* or *Accident*, to the *Folly* or *Carelesness* of Persons only, to any *Cause* rather than the *true one?* Certainly no other Account can be given of such a Spirit as this in Men, than that they are unwilling to part with their Sins, and hate to be reformed. *Be not deceived, God is not mocked* r. The Providence of God, and that for wise and just Reasons, is concerned in all Events. *Shall there be Evil in the City and the Lord hath not done it* s*? Thus saith the Lord, because thy Sins were increased I have done these Things unto thee* t. Shall we not wisely *consider* of our Doings, in this our *Day* of *Adversity*, whereby we have provoked an holy and righteous God to discover such severe Marks of his Displeasure against us? This will lead us on to the next Particular.

q Psal. xlii. 7.   r Gal. vi. 7.   s Amos iii. 6.
t Jer. xxx. 12—15.

III.

III Let us reckon it our indispensable Duty to *confess* our Sins, be grieved for them, and *turn* unto the Lord.

The excellent Example of pious *Ezra* demands our Imitation. *I fell on my Knees and spread out my Hands unto the Lord my God, and said, O my God, I am ashamed, and blush to lift up my Face unto thee my God, for our Iniquities are increased over our Heads, and our Trespasses grown up unto the Heavens* ". Confession of our Sins to God is included in the very Nature of true Repentance. *I said I will confess my Transgressions unto the Lord* [x]. It ought to lie much at our Hearts, that we have a true and genuine *Sorrow* for our Sins, even that *Sorrow which worketh Repentance to Salvation not to be repented of* [y]. If we remain insensible of our manifold Transgressions, unaffected with them, and are not ashamed before God on the Account of them, it must argue an uncommon Degree of Impiety. *Were they ashamed when they had committed Abomination? Nay, they were not at all ashamed, neither could they blush* [z]. Hardened Creatures! Can we forbear Blushing under a deep Sense of our Sins? Let us dread to have that grievous Complaint

---

" Ezra ix 5, 6. [x] Psal. xxxii. 5. [y] 2 Cor vii. 10. [z] Jer. vi. 15.

lodged against us mentioned by the Prophet, *No Man repented him of his Wickedness, saying, What have I done* [a]? On the contrary, it should be the Language of our Hearts, We have greatly offended thee, O God, *Wherefore we abhor our selves, and repent in Dust and Ashes* [b]. Being thus by divine Grace brought into a penitent Frame, let us take hold of this happy Opportunity, in the most serious and solemn Manner, to renounce all our Sins, and to lay our selves under the strongest Resolutions of Amendment. When King *Hezekiah* was considering and grieving for the Distresses of the People occasioned by their Sins, he gave them, and others also, yea, *all Persons*, whether in the most -----d or *meanest* Station in Life, an excellent *Pattern* what ought to be done: *Now it is in my Heart to make a Covenant with the Lord God of* Israel, *that his fierce Wrath may turn away from us* [c]. Let us, in the Strength of God, enter our solemn Protest against all Manner and Kinds of Sin, and purpose without Delay to become the Servants of the most high God. Is it not high Time that we give Proof of the Reality of our Repentance by our becoming an obedient People? *Thus saith*

[a] Jer. viii. 6.   [b] Job xlii. 6.   [c] 2 Chron xxix. 10.

the Lord of Hosts, amend your Ways and your Doings. Trust ye not in lying Words, the Temple of the Lord, the Temple of the Lord, the Temple of the Lord, are these[c]; and from hence conclude, that *we are delivered* to do any *Abominations.* Surely no extravagant *Zeal* for *Parties, Principles, Places,* or different *Modes* of Worship, will ever atone for, or justify us in any *immoral Practices.* Whatever *Profession* a Man makes, though the most *pure;* whatever *Church* a Person is a Member of, though the best constituted in the World, yet if he *lives* not conformable to the Gospel of Christ, his *Profession* is vain, his *Faith* is also vain. *Know ye not, that to whom ye yield your selves Servants to obey, his Servants ye are to whom ye obey; whether of Sin unto Death, or of Obedience unto Righteousness*[d]. All our Hopes of Heaven will prove *delusive,* and we shall but flatter our selves with our own *Deceivings,* unless by *Holiness* of Heart and Life, by Faith in Christ, and Obedience to him, we become a People prepared for the Lord.

Now for our Encouragement to a penitent Confession of our Sins, and that we may turn unto the Lord with all our Heart, we are assured that Christ *is exalt-*

[c] Jer. vii. 3, 10.   [d] Rom. vi. 16.

ed to be a *Prince and a Saviour, for to give Repentance unto* Israel, *and Forgiveness of Sins* [e], and that *if we confess our Sins he is faithful and just to forgive us our Sins* [f]. And being thus happily ranked among the *Penitent* and *pardoned,* though our outward Condition may be low and mean, we may however *rejoice in the Lord, and joy in the God of our Salvation.* Yea, moreover, this is the most likely Method that can be taken by us to engage God's kind Thoughts towards us, and to have temporal Blessings laid up in store for us. Then may we hope to see the Scales of Divine Providence happily turned in our Favour, as in the Words of the Prophet *Jeremiah, And it shall come to pass, that like as I have watched over them to pluck up, and to break down, and to throw down, and to destroy, and to afflict; so will I watch over them, to build, and to plant, saith the Lord* [g].

IV. Let us take great Care that we justify God in all his *Proceedings* against us, how afflictive soever they are either in their *Nature* or *Consequences.*

Should we grow *fretful* and *uneasy* we shall add both to our *Calamity* and Guilt, and instead of *lightning* our Burden render

[e] Acts v. 31. [f] 1 John i. 9. [g] Jer. xxxi. 28.

it the *heavier*. To be patient and submissive under the correcting Hand of God, is a *Duty* so important, that he will by no means dispense with it; not only his own *Glory*, but our real *Good*, are so nearly concerned herein, that his Jealousy for his own *Honour*, and his tender Regard for our *Happiness*, engage him to insist upon it. Though we may humbly plead with God, and *talk with him of his Judgments* [h], yet we must not dare to allow of one rebellious Thought, against the sovereign Lord of Heaven and Earth, *who will not give an Account of his Matters* [i]. *Behold, he taketh away, who can hinder him? Who will say unto him, what dost thou* [k] *?*

Deep Silence o'er th' eternal Palace reign'd,
    When thus the King of Heav'n and Earth began;
Go faithful Uriel, *carry this Command*
    To yonder World, inhabited by Man.
Make them know this, that all they have is mine,
    I've only lent, but given Nought to Men;
On my Demand they therefore must resign,
    And All with Gratitude part with again.
But how, and when, is mine, not theirs to say,
I am their sovereign Lord, and will that they obey.

Thus a Reverend Clergymen piously speaks on this our late Calamity, in a

[h] Jer. xii. 1.   [i] Job xxxiii. 13.   [k] Job ix. 12.

Poem entiled, *Directions how to gain by Losses*, p 7

Besides, considering what we have been, what we have done, what we are, and that we have by our Sins often forfeited, not only all the good Things that we have *lost*, but those we have *left*, yea, and our very *Lives* too, nay, have deserved God's *everlasting Displeasure*, how *unreasonable* must every *murmuring* Thought against him be? Yet, though we must not *murmur* we may *sorrow*. Sorrow for our Sins is *inseparable* from our *Duty* as Christians; Sorrow for our Calamities *inseparable* from our *Nature* as Men. *No Affliction for the present is joyous, but grievous;* and we are forbid to *despise the Chastning of the Lord*[1].

That we may be the more *calm* and *easy* under God's Rod, we should take care to revive and cherish those becoming Apprehensions that we *lately* had; whether of the *Majesty* and *Purity* of the Divine Nature; whether of the *evil Nature* of Sin; whether of the *Vanity* and *Emptiness* of the World; whether of the Love and *Favour* of God; whether of the *Importance* and *Consolation* of a Claim through Christ to a better World, till these *Thoughts* be fixed

---
[1] Heb. xii. 5—11.

in our Minds, and engraven on our Hearts.

V. Guard against the over-bearing Power of worldly Cares

I am sure this Piece of Advice can neither be *improper* in it self, nor *impertinent* to our Case, seeing our blessed Lord himself (who well knew the Nature of Men and Things) has charged us that we *take Heed to our selves, lest at any Time our Hearts be overcharged with the Cares of this Life*[m]. *We particularly* have seen so much of the transitory Nature of all earthly Things, that one would think we had need *now* to put some *Force* upon our selves, in order to apply to the Concerns of Time with that Diligence and Industry as we *ought* to do; but alas! so hardly are we cured of our *Over-fondness* for this World, that some, perhaps, are in more *danger* of over-doing than ever. So uneasy are their *Losses* to them, that they impatiently desire an Increase of their worldly Substance, and thereupon are inclined to prosecute this *Design*, even with a sinful and destructive *Eagerness*. That we may avoid this Extreme let us conscientiously observe the Words of the Apostle, *And having Food and*

[m] Luke xxi. 34.

Raiment let us be therewith content. But they that will be rich fall into Temptations and a Snare, and into many foolish and hurtful Lusts, which drown Men in Destruction and Perdition[n].

Many Arguments may be urged to preserve us from the Power of a sinful Carefulness; as, that it carries its own *Punishment* along with it, hereby the Mind is so *ruffled* that the Man becomes *uneasy* to himself and all about him. It implies a *reproachful Distrust* of the *Goodness* of God, who is tenderly concerned for the Welfare of his Creatures. It is also altogether *useless* and unprofitable, for *which of you by taking Thought can add one Cubit unto his Stature*[o]? Moreover, will it not be very *ungrateful* in any of the sincere Disciples of Christ, should they indulge a *carking Solicitude*, when he has not only kindly warned them against it, but assured them of his abundant Care? *Therefore take no Thought, saying, what shall we eat? Or, what shall we drink? Or, wherewithal shall we be clothed? For your heavenly Father knoweth that ye have Need of all these Things*[p]. May these Considerations effectually prevail upon us to cast all our Care on God, *for he careth for us*[q].

[n] 2 Tim. vi 8, 9. [o] Matth. vi. 27. [p] Matth. vi. 31, 32. [q] 1 Pet. v. 7.

I cannot but have a special Compassion on some who may be in danger of the contrary Extreme to this; for *lately* such was their Condition, that they were furnished with all the *Necessaries* and *Conveniencies* of Life, but now such a sad *Change* is made, so low are they reduced, and so small their Hopes of recovering their former *Station* in Life, that they are even tempted to grow *desperate*, and to give up themselves to *Looseness* and *Extravagancy*. Think a little, will this make your Case better! Will it not make it vastly worse? Because you cannot live in this World in as flourishing a Manner as once you presumed you should, will you therefore live more like *Beasts* than *Men?* Because you have lost *this World*, will you therefore, instead of being excited to think of, and make sure of a *better*, make sure of neither? What, because you have lost your worldly Treasure, will you therefore (as an unavoidable Consequence of your Impieties) *treasure up for your selves Wrath against the Day of Wrath* [r]? For God's sake act not such an unreasonable self-destructive Part; rather learn from all your worldly Losses and Disappointments to

[r] Rom. ii. 5.

think of, and provide for a World where you can meet with none.

This will lead me to another Piece of Advice.

VI. Esteem an *Interest in Christ* as a Matter of the greatest Moment.

An *Eternity*, an awful Eternity, an happy or a miserable Eternity, depends upon it, *For other Foundation can no Man lay, than that is laid, which is Jesus Christ*[s]. Those that by Faith and Repentance, Love and Obedience, are interested in Christ Jesus, whatever *Losses* they may sustain, whatever *Calamities* they may suffer, will not only escape a World of *endless Misery*, but reach safe to a World of *consummate Felicity*. For *whosoever believeth on him shall not perish but have eternal Life* [t]. Think of this with the greatest *Seriousness*; pray for it with the utmost *Earnestness*; give no Rest to your selves, till your Hopes of Heaven be securely settled on this *Foundation*.

That we may not *neglect* this great Salvation wrought out for us by Christ Jesus, but may honour, love, live unto him, and depend by Faith upon him as an All-sufficient and Precious Redeemer, let us so-

---

[s] 1 Cor. iii. 11.   [t] John iii. 15.

lemnly confider what he has *done* and *suffered* for us; he left Heaven, he became a Man of Sorrows, he endured the Wrath of God, he died on the accurfed Tree, he arofe from the Dead (a Matter of Fact, feen and attefted by above *five Hundred* Perfons at once [x]) *He is gone into Heaven it self, now to appear in the Prefence of God for us* [y]. He is there *preparing a Place* [z] for every one of his faithful Difciples, and will come again and receive them to himfelf, that where he is there they may be alfo. Moft *engaging Confiderations!* Enough to attract our Hearts for ever to himfelf, and to fix us for ever in his Service. *May the Love of Chrift conftrain us, becaufe we thus judge, that if one died for all then were all Dead; and that he died for all, that they which live fhould not henceforth live unto themfelves* (no truly, God forbid, this would be the bafeft Ingratitude poffible) *but unto him which died for them, and rofe again* [a]. Oh, refufe him not, I befeech you, for *how fhall ye efcape if ye neglect fo great Salvation* [b]? And if you fhould, will it not *be more tolerable for the Land of* Sodom *in the Day of Judgment than for you* [c]?

[x] 1 Cor. xv. 6.   [y] Heb. ix. 24.   [z] John xiv. 3.   [a] 2 Cor. v. 14, 15.   [b] Heb. ii. 3.
[c] Matth. xi. 24.

VII.

VII. Let nothing short of *Regeneration* by the Spirit of God satisfy or content us, as an Evidence of our Interest in Christ.

Were we fully to describe the Nature of *Regeneration*, or being *born of God*, which the Scripture assures us is necessary to Salvation (*For except a Man be born again he cannot see the Kingdom of God*[d]) it would render this Treatise too large. However, that such a *necessary* and *important* Change[e] may

[d] John iii. 3.

[e] Archbishop *Tillotson*, in his Fourth Volume has several Sermons on this important Point of Christianity. The Title to his Sermons is this, *The Nature of Regeneration, and its Necessity in order to Justification and Salvation*. In *Page* 159, &c. he treats of two Things from that Phrase of a *new Creature*, as,

1. "The Greatness of this Change.
2. "That it is effected and wrought by a Divine "Power.

1. "The Greatness of this Change. It is called "Καινὴ κτίσις, *a new Creation*, as if the Christian "Doctrine firmly entertained and believed, did, as "it were, mould and fashion Men over again, trans-"forming them into a quite other sort of Persons than "what they were before, and made such a Change "in them as the Creating Power of God did, in "bringing this beautiful and orderly Frame of Things "out of their dark and rude *Chaos*. Thus the Apo-"stle represents it, 2 *Cor*. iv. 6. *God who commanded* "*the Light*, &c. His Second Particular is this,

2. "This Change is effected and wrought by a "Divine Power, of the same Kind with that which "created the World, and raised up Christ Jesus from "the

may not be passed over in silence, I will take Notice briefly, That it consists in having our *Minds* enlighten'd by the Spirit of God. Hereby we are enabled more clearly to apprehend the spotless *Purity* of God, the *Beauty* and *Excellency* of real Religion, the malignant and destructive *Nature* of Sin, as that which is directly repugnant to God's perfect *Holiness.* Those that are *sanctified in Christ Jesus* [f] *are filled with the Knowledge of his Will, in all Wisdom and spiritual Understanding* [g]. Regeneration includes in it a Change in the *Will.* Where this obtains the *Dominion* of Sin is broken, and those vicious *Lusts* and *Appetites* which were once predominant are conquered and subdued. *Sin no longer reigns in our mortal Bodies* [h], but we *through the Spirit do mortify the Deeds of the Body* [i]; and are will-

"the Dead, two great and glorious Instances of the
"Divine Power, and to these the Scripture frequently alludes, when it speaks of this *new Creation.* Like as Christ was raised, *&c.* Rom vi. 4.
"Eph i 19, 20. *And that ye may know what is the exceeding Greatness of his Power,* &c. So that our
"*Renovation,* and being made *new Creatures,* is an
"Instance of the same glorious Power which exerted
"it self in the first Creation of Things, and in the
"Resurrection of our Lord Jesus Christ from the Dead;
"but not altogether after the same Manner, as (says
"he) I shall shew under the next Head."

[f] 1 Cor 1. 2.   [g] Col. 1. 9.   [h] Rom. vi. 12.
[i] Rom. viii 13.

ing

ing to have *respect to all God's Commandments* [k], and to submit to all his providential *Dispensations*, be they ever so severe, or how nearly soever they may affect us. *Regeneration*, as to its Fruits, implies farther, a growing *Regulation* of our *Affections* and *Passions*, whereby they are withdrawn from *unlawful Objects*, moderated as to *lawful* ones, and set chiefly on those *Things which are above, where Christ sitteth on the right Hand of God* [l]. In a Word, *being sanctified by the Holy Ghost*, we shall *put off the old Man with his Deeds, and put on the new Man which is renewed in Knowledge after the Image of him that created him* [m], i. e. we shall be Persons very different from what we once were; and that as to our *Apprehensions, Esteem, Inclinations, Choice, Resolutions, Pursuits, Expectations*, and *Dependance*. Happy they who are taught of God, and made *Vessels unto Honour, sanctified and meet for the Master's Use, and prepared unto every good Work* [n]. I shall say no more on this Head. I choose rather to refer you to a valuable Treatise of *being Born again*, now in its Thirteenth Edition, published not long since by the Reverend *S. Wright*, D. D. and at the Request of

[k] Psalm cxix. 6.   [l] Col. iii. 1.   [m] Col. iii. 9, 10.
[n] 2 Tim. ii. 21.

some

some Persons of the *established Church* who heard him preach on that *Subject*. I have received many of them from the worthy Author since the Fire (as well as some other Books) and have distributed them among the Sufferers, as desired.

VIII. Strictly and conscientiously observe the *Lord's Day*, and be found in the constant Discharge of those Duties that Christ has enjoined us in his Word

Remember the Sabbath Day to keep it holy°. Good God, incline our Hearts to keep this Law. That we may observe this Day as *Holy* unto the Lord, let us begin it *alone* with God, with serious *Meditation*, solemn *Reading* his Word, and with secret and fervent *Prayer* Then let every *Master* or *Head* of Families call them together for some Acts of *social Worship*, by this Means we and our Houses shall be best disposed to wait upon God in his publick *Appointments* that he may *teach us his Ways, and that we may walk in his Paths* ᴾ. Though a proper Portion of Time may be allotted for our bodily *Refreshment*, yet all Manner of *Excess*, should on this Day especially, be carefully avoided, as that which would be peculiarly offensive to God; nor

° Exod. xx. 8.   ᴾ Isai. ii. 3.

should we dare to feast our *perishing Bodies* to the starving or hurt of our *precious Souls*. We should conscientiously avoid such *Entertainments*, and the making or receiving such *Visits* as break in upon the religious *Order* of our Families, or that prevent us from a constant Attendance on publick Worship. When this is over, then let us return with the several *Branches* of our Families to our own Houses, and employ the Remains of the *Lord's Day* either in useful *Instructions* and *Exhortations*, in pious and profitable *Conversation*, and in the proper Acts of *Family* and *secret Worship*. And as no Part of this *sacred Day* should be laid out in unnecessary *Business*, so none of it must be wasted away in *impertinent* or vain Pursuits, these having a natural Tendency to deface any good Impressions that have been made upon us whilst attending the Service of God according to his Appointments. Thus our blessed Saviour observes of some, *who, when they have heard, go forth and are choaked with Cares, and Riches, and Pleasures of this Life, and bring no Fruit to Perfection* [q]. Besides, what Persons get by following their *Employments* on the *Sabbath*, is put into a *Bag with Holes*; or if it mixes with their honest Gains it

[p] Luke viii. 14.

is like to bring a *Curse*, a *Blast*, on all the rest. Such as find their *Pleasure* on this Day, will soon have their *Pleasure* turned into *Pain* and Uneasiness, in this World or in the next, for God is a jealous God. *Remember the Sabbath Day to keep it holy. Six Days shalt thou labour and do all thy Work, but the seventh Day is the Sabbath of the Lord thy God; in it thou shalt not do any Work, thou, nor thy Son, nor thy Daughter, thy Man-servant, nor thy Maid-servant, nor thy Cattle, nor thy Stranger that is within thy Gates; for in six Days the Lord made Heaven and Earth, the Sea, and all that in them is, and rested the seventh Day. Wherefore the Lord blessed the Sabbath Day and hallowed it* [r]. *Thus saith the Lord, Take heed to your selves, and bear no Burden on the Sabbath Day, neither do ye any Work, but hallow ye the Sabbath Day, as I commanded your Fathers* [s]. *If thou turn away thy Foot from the Sabbath, from doing thy Pleasure on my holy Day, and call the Sabbath a Delight, the holy of the Lord, honourable, and shalt honour him, not doing thine own Ways, nor finding thine own Pleasure, nor speaking thine own Words. Then shalt thou delight thy self in the Lord, and I will cause thee to ride upon the high Places of the Earth, and feed thee with*

---

[r] Exod. xx. 8—12.   [s] Jer. xvii. 21, 22.

the Heritage of Jacob *thy Father, for the Mouth of the Lord hath spoken it* [t]. And shall we not hear and obey the Voice of the Lord? Especially too, when our Lord Jesus Christ himself has said, *Think not that I am come to destroy the Law or the Prophets, I am not come to destroy but to fulfill* [u].

Esteem

---

[t] Isai. lviii. 13, 14.   [u] Matth. v. 17.

Though our blessed Saviour does not in this Sermon of his take particular Notice of the Innovations made upon, and the superstitious Abuse of the Fourth Commandment, as he does concerning others, yet this he does, and at a more convenient Season afterwards, and that more than once. At one Time in Vindication of his Disciples when they *plucked the Ears of Corn*, Matt. xii. 1. At another Time, when he healed the Man which had his Hand withered, *Matth.* xii. 10. From the former Case, or on a like Occasion, mentioned by St. *Mark*, Chap. ii. 23, &c. our Saviour not only freely condemns the superstitious Abuse of the Sabbath, but *ver.* 27, 28. there tells them the Reasons of it. *And he said unto them, the Sabbath was made for Man,* i. e. for the Good and Benefit of Man, *and not Man for the Sabbath,* i. e. no Man is obliged so to sanctify the Sabbath as thereby to subject himself to any real or pernicious Inconveniencies, or to prevent him from other Services when the Nature and Necessity of Things require it, as in the Cases of War, Fire, Sickness, or the like. *Therefore the Son of Man is Lord also of the Sabbath,* i. e. has not only a Power and Authority devolved on him to discharge Men from any superstitious or self-injurious Regard to the Sabbath, which some have taught as necessary, and thereby rendered the Observation of it grievous and burdensome,

Esteem not such an Observation of the Lord's Day tedious. Say not, *What a Weariness is it? When will the Sabbath be gone,*

some, but has also such a Dominion granted to him, that he may, if he sees fit, as *Lord of the Sabbath*, alter the very Day it self, which is highly probable our Lord did afterward, as the most effectual Way *at once* to cure Men of a superstitious Observation of it. The Probability of this is not small, as will appear, if we will allow our selves to consider, that our Lord rose from the Dead on the first Day of the Week, and then appeared to his Disciples, and again, after eight Days he came and stood in the midst of them, *John* xx. 19, 26. whereby he signalized this Day, and made the Memory of it precious to his Followers. Besides, the *Practice* of the first Disciples of our Lord (who were most like to know his Mind and Will, and because without the Knowledge of his Will this was not like to have been their Practice) makes this Change of the Day highly probable, for this was the Day when they, after Christ's Resurrection, met together for publick Worship, as we read, *And upon the first Day of the Week, when the Disciples came together to break Bread,* Paul *preached unto them,* Acts xx. 7. This Day also was observed as Holy unto the Lord by the primitive Christians in the earliest Ages of Christianity, none dispute it. We read, 1 *Cor.* xvi. 2. upon the first Day of the Week, when they are supposed to assemble together, which I think one may venture to affirm, without any doubt, was for the publick Worship of God. Moreover, as one grand Ordinance of Christianity is termed the *Lord's Supper*, 1 Cor. xi. 20. so is this the *Lord's Day*, Rev. 1. 10. emphatically so called, it being the Day which he seems to have appropriated to himself, and appointed for his Service.

gone, that we may set forth Wheat [x] ? Sabbaths strictly observed will not sit uneasy in dying Hours, nor would they now, were there a serious and pious Spirit. Would not the constant uninterrupted Services of the Saints in Heaven (for they never cease from serving God) be burdensome to such Persons, could they possibly be admitted there, who think it much, if not more than enough, to spend an Hour in

To which we might add, that none, I think, can fairly or justly infer from the Change of the Day, the abolishing or destroying the Law it self concerning the Sabbath, seeing all the Ends of that Law can be as well answered by our strict and pious Regard had to this Day as to the other. The Reasons for the Observation of the Sabbath, inserted in the Precept it self (though other Reasons were afterwards added for the Keeping the Sabbath, which were peculiar to the *Jews*) are of equal Force on us now as on former Generations, such as a pious Remembrance, and constant Declaration hereby of our Belief, that God created the World in six Days, and rested the seventh, only with this Difference, that we keep the first Day and not the seventh, whereby we not only as certainly and solemnly commemorate and declare our Belief of God's having created the World and resting from his Works, but hereby also we solemnly remember, and declare our Belief of Christ's rising from the Dead on the first Day, when he compleated the great Work of our Redemption, and then entered into his Rest, and ceased from his own Works, as God did from his.

[x] Amos viii. 5.

Acts

Acts of publick Worship, and then waste away the other Parts of the Day in minding their *Business*, serving their *Lusts*, or in finding their *Pleasures*? If a right Observation of the *Sabbath* be thought intolerable, it must be ascribed to the Perverseness and Earthliness of Men's Hearts, and not to any Severity in the Institution it self; no, that was kind and gracious, with a Design to promote our present *Good* and *Peace*, and to render us more *meet* for an *eternal Sabbath* in Heaven. *There remaineth therefore a Rest*, σαββατισμὸς, a Sabbatism, or keeping of a Sabbath, *to the People of God* [y]. They that like and love, that strictly observe, and conscientiously improve God's Sabbaths now, are Persons rightly disposed for the Employments of the heavenly World above.

Should I not be so happy as to prevail on some to make Conscience of a *due Regard* to the Sabbath; too many 'tis to be feared will still prophane it; yet I would please my self with the Hope that such as are in *Authority*, or of *Rank* and *Figure* among us, will by their good *Example*, and *pious Care*, prevent any open and scandalous *Profanation* of this *sacred Time*, nor would I have any think, that *Religion* is

[y] Heb. iv. 9.

to be confined within the *Limits* of a *Sabbath*, no, we ought so to *sanctify* God's *Sabbaths*, that we may learn to behave the better, both towards God and Men, on every other Day, we shall, otherwise, be justly chargeable with meer *Formality* in *Religion*, contrary to the very Nature and Design of it. We are not only to worship and serve God on the Lord's Day, but every Day of our Lives. *Secret Prayer* should be esteemed a Duty of daily Revolution. The Duty it self our Saviour has solemnly and kindly obliged us to the Performance of. *But thou, when thou prayest, enter into thy Closet, and when thou hast shut thy Door, pray to thy Father which is in secret*[z]. Yea, we should be without Excuse, if every *Family* met not together daily at the Throne of Grace to implore God's favourable Regards, and to commit themselves to his Care and Protection. I should rejoice for your sakes, and for the sake of Religion too, to see that Day, when every *Habitation* may become a *House of Prayer*. The *Reasonableness* and *Usefulness* of these Duties, as well as our *Obligation* to the Performance of them, will be always evident, while we have *Personal* and *Family Sins* to confess and bewail; *Blessings* to

[z] Matth. vi. 6.

ask, and *numberless Mercies* to give God Thanks for. Have we *new Habitations?* I would to God we had *new Hearts* too. Then with an humble Confidence we might pray with the *Psalmist*, *Return, O Lord, how long! and let it repent thee concerning thy Servants. O satisfy us early with thy Mercy, that we may rejoice and be glad all our Days. Make us glad according to the Days wherein thou hast afflicted us, and the Years wherein we have seen Evil. Let thy Work appear unto thy Servants, and thy Glory unto their Children. And let the Beauty of the Lord our God be upon us, and establish thou the Work of our Hands upon us, yea, the Work of our Hands establish thou it* [a].

But before I leave this Particular, suffer me to mind you of one *important Duty* more, I mean the constant and serious *Reading* the *holy Scriptures*.

Among other Complaints that were made soon after the Fire, I well remember this was one, not only our *Habitations*, and our *Places* of *Worship* are demolished, but alas! our *Bibles* too are burnt in the Flames. The Occasion of the Complaint was sad, yet the Complaint it self carried a good Intimation with it, so that one could not forbear hoping, if such Persons were again

---

[a] Psal. xc. 13, &c.

supply'd with this *sacred Volume*, they would not only barely look into it, but take God's Word for a *Lamp unto their Feet and a Light unto their Path*. You know, that upon Application made to some well disposed Gentlemen in *London*, *Bibles* were sent to some Persons of this Town, which were with *Pleasure* distributed by them, and *thankfully* received by you. Now will it not be very ungrateful both to God and Man, should you neglect diligently to read and meditate on them? But I would hope better Things of many of you, and such as *accompany Salvation, though I thus speak*. I could mention (was there need of it) many Arguments to press you to the Performance of this Duty. The blessed God took Compassion on a blind and ignorant World, and *at sundry Times, and in divers Manners, spake in Time past unto the Fathers, by the Prophets· And hath in these last Days spoken unto us by his Son* [b]; and has kindly taken Care that his Mind and Will thus made known unto us should be committed to Writing, and handed down to us. Besides, are not the Scriptures designed to be the Rule and *Standard* of our *Faith* and *Manners*? The Rule by which we are to *live*, and by which we are to be *judg'd*? In

[b] Heb. i. 1, 2.

a Word, do they not contain all those *Doctrines, Precepts, Prohibitions* and *Promises*, needful to our *Direction, Admonition, Consolation*, and eternal *Salvation? All Scripture is given by Inspiration of God, and is profitable for Doctrine, for Reproof, for Correction, for Instruction in Righteousness, that the Man of God may be perfect, throughly furnished unto all good Works* c.

IX.

c 2 Tim iii. 16, 17.

That the diligent and careful *Perusal* of the *Scriptures* would be of great Service to us, one may be sure, had we no other Reason to think so than the following one, *viz.* that the known and open Enemies of the Cause of *Christ* and his *Kingdom* are such avowed Adversaries to this Practice. For they, you know (as what they rightly judge would best tend to serve their *dark Purposes*) take out of the Hands of the People those *Weapons* of our Christian Warfare, which though not *carnal*, are *mighty, through God, to the pulling down the strong Holds of Satan*, 2 Cor x 4. These *divine Oracles* would make us *wiser than our Enemies*, Psal. cxix. 98 were they ever with us. I have many Times thought, even with Shame and Surprize, what Pains and Expence the *Romish Church* is at to propagate the *Christian Faith*, as they are pleased to term theirs; when, in Truth, many of their *Doctrines* are a Reproach to Christianity. To name no other here than these two, *viz.* That NO FAITH IS TO BE KEPT WITH HERETICKS, meaning Protestants. And THAT IF THEY KILL US THEY DO GOD SERVICE. *Doctrines* that could never come from God, for *God is Love*, but must be from their Father *the Devil* They have a watchful and *greedy Eye* on this *happy Island*, with restless Labour they endeavour to proselyte many

among

IX. Let *Love* to God, and *Benevolence* to Men, be a governing *Principle* in our Breast.

As these are Duties in their Nature most important, so those Favours we have received from both in our afflicted Cir-

among us, nor have they been altogether successless in their Attempts. To prevent the spreading of this Plague amongst us it would please me much if this following proper *Antidote*, with others, was provided, *viz* that those who have it in their Power would take effectual Care, by some *legal Provision*, that Bibles printed on *good Paper*, and in a *fair Character*, may come as *cheap* as possible, that every *Family* in *Great Britain* may have *one* at least in their Houses.

I would here also take Notice further of an Observation I made some Years past, on the Reading a Volume published by *Tho Ward*, in which he has artfully and wickedly burlesqued the glorious Reformation from Popery. Among other Things, like a *cunning Priest*, he exposes the good old laudable *Custom* of Persons bringing their *Bibles* with them to *Church*. *Fas est & ab Hoste doceri*. A good Custom, I wish its Revival, and that all *Protestant Ministers* would, in their *Sermons* (as Occasion requires) not only mention the *Words of Scripture*, but the *Chapter* and *Verse* also, by this Means the *People* would become intimately acquainted with their Bibles, than which, nothing whatsoever would more effectually establish Persons in the glorious Cause of *Protestantism*, and more effectually prevent the spreading of *cruel* and *enslaving Popery*. My great Veneration for the holy Bible, and my true Concern for the Protestant Cause (which, no Doubt, is the Cause of God) inclined me to insert this Paragraph in the Margin.

cumstances,

cumstances, peculiarly oblige us, to the Observance of them, as I shall shew more at large under the next Head.

Love to God, and Love to our Neighbour, these two include all the Parts and Branches of Religion. *Thou shalt love the Lord thy God with all thy Heart, and with all thy Soul, and with all thy Mind. This is the first and great Commandment, and the second is like unto it, Thou shalt love thy Neighbour as thy self. On these two Commandments hang all the Law and the Prophets* [d].

First, Love to God.

Nothing is more reasonable, than that we love God, the God that made us, the Saviour that redeem'd us; that Being from whom all our Blessings descend; for *every good Gift, and every perfect Gift, is from above* [e]. If we are happily and powerfully influenc'd by this Divine Principle, namely, Love to God, we shall be sincere and cheerful in our Obedience to him. So far then will it be, from being an *Uneasiness* to us, to serve and honour God, in every *Capacity* and *Station* of Life, that we shall not be satisfied till this be our constant Temper. *For this is the Love of God, that we keep his Commandments, and his Commandments are not grievous* [f].

[d] Matth. xxii. 37. [e] James i. 17. [f] 1 John v. 3.

Secondly,

Secondly, *Love to our Neighbour.*

When this prevails in us we shall be readily disposed to fill up those Duties we owe to each other as *Fellow-Creatures*, and *Christians*. If Love be wanting, our Hearts will soon be filled with those *cruel Vices* which draw after them many great and sore Calamities. When *Wrath*, *Hatred*, and *Envy* reign in the Heart, what less can be expected than *Confusion and every evil Work*. Would it not be very *unseemly*, and Matter of *Reproach*, for a People that are involved in one *common Distress*, to be full of *Anger*, *Rancour*, *Wrath* and *Malice*? Such a *savage Temper* as this would render us most *contemptible* in the Eye of God and all wise and good Men. Let therefore all *hard Speeches*, all *ill Usage* of one another, all *opprobrious Names*, which tend to irritate our *Passions*, and to excite contemptible Thoughts of others; let all *Ill-will*, and *contemptuous Shiness*, from henceforth cease, and be no more, let each of us rather turn our *Resentments* against our Sins, and look upon our common Affliction as a warm Incentive to *Benevolence*. And if we are yet inclined to *provoke* one another, let it be only *to Love and good Works* [g]. *Let us love as Brethren.* For the Kingdom of

---

[g] Heb. x. 24.

God

God is not Meat and Drink, but Righteousness and Peace, and Joy in the Holy Ghost [h]. We should *endeavour*, as the Apostle exhorts us, *to keep the Unity of the Spirit in the Bond of Peace. There is one Body and one Spirit, even as ye are called in one Hope of your Calling. One Lord, one Faith, one Baptism, one God and Father of all, who is above all, and through all, and in us all* [i].

An *human Law* is made with this Preamble to it, for *determining Differences*, &c. But that we may save those *Gentlemen* therein nominated, and our selves too, the Trouble of determining any more *Differences*, let us prevent them by our conscientious Observance of the great *Law of Love*. *Love worketh no ill to his Neighbour, therefore Love is the fulfilling of the Law* [k]. *Love*, God-like Virtue indeed! It is pity it was not a *regent Principle* in every Breast; then not only all base *Ill-nature* and diabolical *Malice* and *Envy* would fall before it, but even lesser *Strifes* and *Debates* too, and many would be the great and valuable Effects and Consequences thereof. If Love reign'd in our Hearts, this would incline us to be *tender* one of another; to yield to any Thing *reasonable*

[h] Rom. xiv. 7. [i] Eph. iv. 3, &c. [k] Rom. xiii. 10.

for Peace sake, to deny our selves in some *lesser Matters* that we may do another a *greater Kindness*; to be ready to do all *good Offices*, and to study each others *Happiness*. This would render us more like the Inhabitants of the upper *World*, where *perfect Love* reigns, and where God, who is *Love*, dwells.

He that wants these, *viz*. *Love to God*, and *Love to his Neighbour*, wants the very *Essence* of Religion. And as we would hope shortly to reach that most agreeable *State* above, where Love is in *Perfection*, *universal* and *everlasting*, let us practically regard the Charge of the Apostle. *Put on therefore (as the Elect of God, holy and beloved) Bowels of Mercies, Kindness, Humbleness of Mind, Meekness, Long-suffering. Forbearing one another, and forgiving one another. If any Man have a Quarrel against any, even as Christ forgave you, so also do ye. And above all these Things put on Charity, which is the Bond of Perfectness*[1].

X. We should be abundantly *thankful* to *God* for all Favours received, and truly *grateful* to our *Benefactors*.

Both God and Man have laid us under the particular Obligation of Grati-

[1] Col. iii. 12, &c.

tude. Nothing can be more reasonable, than that the *high Praises of God should be in our Mouth*, who has put it into the Hearts of Men to give so *willingly*, so *liberally*. The most grateful Returns are due to our generous *Benefactors*.

The *Royal Bounty* claims our *first Regards*; and I hope we shall always esteem our selves under peculiar Engagements to the greatest *Loyalty* and Duty, and bound to send up our fervent Prayers to Heaven for our *most gracious Sovereign King* GEORGE, his *Royal* CONSORT, and all the *Royal* FAMILY; That Prosperity and Peace may attend them; and those Blessings be perpetuated to their Posterity as long as the Sun and Moon endure.

The great Benevolence of others also, will, I trust, effectually prevail upon us to pray to that God, who *is able to make all Grace abound towards them*, that they may always have all Sufficiency in all Things; yea, that as they have *sown to the Spirit, they may of the Spirit reap Life everlasting* [m].

Give me leave to add this further Advice in the next Place.

[m] Gal. vi. 8.

XI. Let it lie much at Heart, that we become a People *eminent* for Religion.

The *signal Favours* we have received, and the *severe Calamities* we have endured, and yet feel, are Considerations that should add double Weight to this Admonition. We should, in one Case, discover our grateful Sense of Benefits conferred on us both from God and Man, by our being not only *truly*, but *eminently* pious. Nothing is more *pleasing* to God, nor is any Thing like to be more *beneficial* to Men, than when our *Light does so shine before them, that they may see our good Works, and glorify our Father which is in Heaven*[n]. In the other Case, having been cast into the *Fire*, it is fit we should leave our *Dross* behind us. The blessed God kindly intended hereby to refine and purify us. *I will turn my Hand upon thee, and will purely purge away thy Dross, and take away all thy Tin. Afterward thou shalt be called the City of Righteousness, the faithful City*[o]. We ought to be a *Pattern* of prevailing and substantial *Piety* to Places around us. Then may it be said *Happy Blandford!* tho' instructed by the Rod of God's Anger. To this End I heartily wish, that such Persons as are of *Influence* among us of

[n] Matth. v. 16.   [o] Isai i. 25, 26.

every

every *Denomination*, would exert themselves to the utmost of their Power, for reforming us. By this means, at least, open *Immoralities* would be discountenanced, and daring *Offenders* be ashamed. Such a *Method* as this would certainly redound to our *Honour*, and be the most probable Means of our future *Safety* and *Peace*. I leave this to your most serious Thoughts, and beg of God to inspire you with such just and becoming *Sentiments* as may incline you to it.

Finally, Let us live and act as *dying* and *accountable* Creatures.

It is appointed unto Men once to die, and after this the Judgment [p]. We must soon draw our last *Breath*, and shortly stand before the *Bar* of God. Solemn Thoughts indeed! I mention this not to make you sad, but *wise, wise unto Salvation*. Were we never to *die*, never to be *judged*, we might walk after the Vanity of our Mind, and *serve divers Lusts and Pleasures*, nor would our Behaviour on such a Supposition be altogether so unreasonable. Lately we escaped the Flames with our Lives, and found a Place of Refuge; but e'er long no one will be able to deliver himself

[p] Heb. ix. 27.

or Brother from the Power of Death, or to make his Escape in the Day of the Lord's Anger, *viz.* that *universal Burning Day*, when all Nations shall be gathered before him. What *unthinking Creatures* must those be, who will not lay these Things to Heart, who will not now cry for Mercy and Salvation *to God, even the Father of our Lord Jesus Christ, the Father of Mercies*, especially too, when their Neglect here will shortly put them under the sad Necessity of crying to the relentless *Mountains*, and pitiless *Rocks, Fall on us, and hide us from the Face of him that sitteth on the Throne, and from the Wrath of the Lamb*[q]. Say not in thy wicked Heart, *my Lord delayeth his coming*, and thereupon indulge thy self *to eat and drink with the drunken*[r]. *For the Lord is not slack concerning his Promise (as some Men count slackness) but is long-suffering to us-ward, not willing that any should perish, but that all should come to Repentance. But the Day of the Lord will come as a Thief in the Night, in which the Heavens shall pass away with a great Noise, and the Elements shall melt with fervent Heat, the Earth also, and the Works that are therein shall be burnt up. Seeing then that all these Things shall be dissolved, what*

[q] Rev. vi. 16.   [r] Matth. xxiv. 48, 49.

Manner of *Persons* (very different to what many of us now are) *ought we to be in all holy Conversation and Godliness, looking for, and hasting unto the Coming of the Day of God*ˢ. May we be so wise as to *consider our latter End*ᵗ. Think often of giving in our solemn Account before that God *who will judge the Secrets of Men by Jesus Christ,*

ˢ 2 Pet. iii. 9, 10, 11, 12.

ᵗ *N B.* We in this Town have had particular and loud Calls to think of our *latter End* I mean, as by the *sudden* and *violent Death* of many on that Day, when the Town was reduced to Ashes, so by the Death of *many* Persons since, who, either through the *Labour* and *Fatigue,* the *Shocks* and *Surprizes* of that Day, or by their *Losses* then sustained, which stuck too close to them, or by the *Methods* taken since that Time to drown their Sorrows, are gone into another World. To which let me add, the *Removing* of the *Remains* of many of our departed Friends, occasioned by the *Digging* up the Foundations of the old Church, and the *Laying* the Foundation of the new one, so that the Bones of many were either carefully and decently replaced in some *new Graves*, or thrown together, and interred in some *common Heaps*. Many out of *Curiosity*, and others through a kind of decent *Necessity*, have lately seen many Graves opened, and were called to converse with our Dead, which *Circumstance* and *Consequence* of our Calamity ought to be improved by us, and should mind us of that Passage in *Job, I have said to Corruption, thou art my Father, to the Worm, thou art my Mother and my Sister,* Job xvii. 14.

accord-

*according to his Gospel*ᵘ. Let us beg of God to impress our Minds with the powerful and governing *Influences* of these important Truths, that we may be fully determined to take Christ's *Word* for our *Rule*, his *Example* for our *Pattern*; and by *Faith* rely upon him as our only *Lord, Saviour*, and *Advocate*; and his Spirit to *guide, sanctify*, and *comfort* us. Then we may have solid *Rest* and *Peace* in our own Breast; then we need not be afraid to *die*, or to appear before God's awful *Tribunal*; then Death will be our Gain, Christ the *Judge* our *Friend*, and *Heaven* the *Place* of our eternal happy *Abode*. *Blessed are the Dead that die in the Lord*ˣ.

But should we now scoff at, and despise the glorious Gospel of our Lord Jesus Christ, and be ashamed of him, ah! what Horror will seize us, what dreadful Confusion shall we be thrown into when we shall see him (for every Eye shall see him) *Come in the Glory of his Father, with his holy Angels, in flaming Fire, taking Vengeance on them that know not God, and that obey not the Gospel of our Lord Jesus Christ; who shall be punished with everlasting Destruction from the Presence of the Lord, and*

ᵘ Rom. ii. 16.   ˣ Rev. xiv. 13.

from the Glory of his Power; when he shall come to be glorified in his Saints, and to be admired in all them that believe, in that Day.

What more weighty or important Arguments than these can possibly be mentioned to persuade Men to become the Servants of God? Will you lay them to Heart? Oh! let it never be said of any of us, God *gave* us Time and *Space to repent* [y] and we repented not; rather let us be *willing* and *obedient*, that we may find the real Advantage of Religion at present, and reap the everlasting blessed and glorious Consequences thereof in a future State through Jesus Christ our Lord, who is *the Way, and the Truth, and the Life*, for *no Man cometh unto the Father but by him* [z]. *And now I commend you to God, and to the Word of his Grace, which is able to build you up, and to give you an Inheritance among all them which are sanctified* [a].

My sincere Desire of others *Happiness* and *Prosperity* inclines me, before I conclude, to drop a Word or two to the Inhabitants of other Places also. *See what God has done to us;* pass ye to *Tiverton,*

[y] Rev. ii. 21. [z] John xiv. 6. [a] Acts xx. 32.

and

and *see*, think of the Case of *Ramsey*; take these awful Warnings, and read the Words of the Prophet, *Woe to them that are at Ease in* Zion, *pass ye unto* Calneh *and see, and from thence go ye to* Hamath *the great, then go down to* Gath *of the* Philistines, *ye that put far away the evil Day* [b]. Surely when God's *Judgments are in the Earth, the Inhabitants of the World will learn Righteousness* [c]. It well becomes all Persons, diligently to *observe*, and carefully to *improve*, such awakening Calamities which we and others have felt. These a wise Providence seems to have ordered in *different Parts* of the Nation, and about the same Time, that Persons may by them be the more nearly and *deeply* affected. Here are two or three *Witnesses* from different *Quarters*, that God is a God that hates Sin, and will sometimes discover his Resentment against it in this Life, that others may hear and see, and fear, and do not so wickedly. May all *Magistrates* esteem themselves concerned from hence, to exert their best Endeavours to put the Laws in *Execution* for the Suppression of *Immoralities*, which, as they *provoke the Eyes of God's Glory* [d], so they often bring on larger or lesser *Societies* of

[b] Amos vi. 1, 2, 3. [c] Isa. xxvi. 9. [d] Isa. iii. 8.

Men Distresses great and inexpressible. Let *Ministers* take the Warning, be *Ensamples to the Flock*[c]. *Cry aloud, spare not, and shew unto the People their Transgressions and their Sins*[f]. And may the *People* every where piously contribute their *Part* towards a general Reformation, then we may hope *that Goodness and Mercy will follow us all the Days of our Lives.*

We should rejoice (I hope many of us should) if our great *Affliction* may occasion your visible *Reformation* If our *Fall* may prove a Means of your *Standing*. If you who have seen in us a manifest, though sad *Proof* of the uncertain and precarious *Tenure* of earthly *Possessions,* may learn from hence to lay up your Treasure in *Heaven*; yea, as the best Return (that we in our *Circumstances* are capable of making you, for all your *Favours* so generously bestowed upon us) we shall, I hope, think our selves bound in *Conscience* and Gratitude to *pray,* that as our *Sufferings* have excited your great *Compassion,* and unsual *Benevolence,* so they may prove a Means, of exciting in you a just *Dread* and an irreconcilable *Abhorrence* of Sin; and a sincere, zealous and constant *Care* to please God in all Things,

[c] 1 Pet. v. 3.   [f] Isa. lviii. 1.

That

That being made free from Sin, and become Servants to God, ye may have your Fruit unto Holiness, and the End everlasting Life. For the Wages of Sin is Death. But the Gift of God is eternal Life, through Jesus Christ our Lord ᵋ.

ᵋ Rom. vi. 22, 23.

FINIS.

Lightning Source UK Ltd.
Milton Keynes UK
UKOW06f2036080115

244226UK00010B/290/P